THE SAINT FOR THE THIRD MILLENNIUM: THÉRÈSE OF LISIEUX

THE SAINT FOR THE THIRD MILLENNIUM:

THÉRÈSE OF LISIEUX

REV. CHARLES P. CONNOR, Ph.D.

ST PAULS

CA
248.247
Co S

Library of Congress Cataloging-in-Publication Data

Connor, Charles P. (Charles Patrick).
   The Saint for the third millennium : Thérèse of Lisieux / by Charles P. Connor.
       p. cm.
   ISBN-13: 978-0-8189-1244-3
   1. Thérèse, de Lisieux, Saint, 1873-1897.   I. Title.

BX4700.T5C745 2007
282.092—dc22

2006033218

Produced and designed in the United States of America by the
Fathers and Brothers of the Society of St. Paul,
2187 Victory Boulevard, Staten Island, New York 10314-6603
as part of their communications apostolate.

ISBN 13: 978-0-8189-1244-3
ISBN 10: 0-8189-1244-8

Printing Information:

Current Printing - first digit   1   2   3   4   5   6   7   8   9   10

Year of Current Printing - first year shown

2007   2008   2009   2010   2011   2012   2013   2014   2015   2016

TABLE OF CONTENTS

FOREWORD

"In recent times no religious order has been granted such clear graces for Mission as has the Carmelite Order. Such divine favors admonish us and counter recent trends in the world and the Church. In an era of churchly projects and campaigns they call us back to the one thing necessary, to CONTEMPLATION. The well of pure CONTEMPLATION, which is the innermost source and mover of all life in the Church, must either be kept clean or be restored to purity." That quote comes from the Swiss theologian, Fr. Hans Urs von Balthasar, arguably one of the greatest theologians and certainly the most cultured of the twentieth century. The quote explains his special interest in the Saints of Carmel — St. Thérèse of Lisieux and Blessed Elizabeth of the Trinity.

Von Balthasar was a close friend of Pope John Paul II and also of Pope Benedict XVI who wrote a beautiful Apostolic Letter on the recent occasion of the centenary of his birth, where he described him as "a theologian who put his work at the service of the Church because he was convinced that theology is useful only within the context of Catholic practice." "I hope the hundredth anniversary observance will stimulate a revival of interest in the work of von Balthasar." "The example that von Balthasar has left us is rather that of an authentic theologian who had discovered in CONTEMPLATION the coherent action in favor of Christian witness in the world."

Von Balthasar's discovery of St. Thérèse as one of God's most precious gifts ever to the Church, truly justifies her title as the greatest Saint of modern times. He beautifully described her as "one of the ageless Saints of God" who will be relevant to all people, all places and all times, until the Second Coming. I mention all of this to emphasize the absolute importance of the work Fr. Charles Connor is undertaking in presenting us with *The Saint for the Third Millennium: Thérèse of Lisieux*. Let us continue to keep in focus above all that St. Thérèse was a contemplative.

In the new *Catechism of the Catholic Church*, published by Pope John Paul II and the Bishops of the world in 1992, St. Thérèse is the most quoted of all the Saints. Fr. Charles Connor, in the most wonderful way, has entered the scene to show us, in a unique and powerfully readable way, who this little Saint is and how much she can help us in our daily Christian living.

I first saw the unfolding of Fr. Connor's thoughts on St. Thérèse in a thirteen-part series of talks on EWTN (the Global Catholic TV and Radio network). Fr. Connor is an accomplished Catholic theologian and historian, and having seen other excellent TV presentations from him I expected to hear something very special on St. Thérèse and in this I was not to be disappointed. I listened spellbound to the entire presentation, spread over a few months — a total of almost seven hours of St. Thérèse — and I was so pleased that EWTN decided to encore the program later. Speaking subsequently with Fr. Connor, I was in no sense surprised when he told me that Alba House had invited him to publish his talks in book form.

St. Thérèse happens to be one of the most written-about

Saints in the history of the Church. Unfortunately, in the earlier years some of the writings, however well meaning, tended not to really understand her and gave a false or incomplete picture of the Saint. Since the late forties, however, some powerful commentaries on her life and spirituality have appeared. Fr. Connor includes all these great writers in his very extensive Bibliography and very importantly, apart from his own deep reflections, has distilled the very best of their thinking into this new beautiful book. The book truly lives up to its title. In eleven beautifully crafted chapters we follow Thérèse from the cradle to the grave while taking in the themes that mean so much to Thérèse and to us — faith, blind trust, total love, how to pray, how to conquer pessimism, the Eucharist and the priesthood and devotion to Our Lady. The final chapter describes how and why she was named a Doctor of the Church, one of only thirty-three Saints so chosen in its entire history.

Fr. Connor begins by giving us a masterly description of the events preceding the final quarter of the nineteenth century as a way of best understanding the time in which St. Thérèse grew up. Looking at the world in which she lived he prepares us to examine more closely the person she was. We are brought into intimate contact with the principal details of her young life within the family and we readily see why her saintly parents, Venerable Louis and Zélie Martin, are, hopefully, soon to be beatified. Thérèse sums up her whole family background when she says "God gave me a father and mother more worthy of heaven than of earth."

In Chapter III, "The 'Little Way' of Confidence and Love," Thérèse makes all of us pause and consider our own inadequacies, our own failures in our ongoing attempts to love and serve God and she makes us realize that God loves us in spite of ourselves, in spite of our weaknesses and sins. We see how Thérèse planned out her entire life. She taught, judged and chose her path calmly with great serenity and clarity of vision. What must be taken very seriously is our growth in holiness and love of God. Fr. Connor makes the astute observation that Thérèse promised to keep working until time is no more — what could possibly make any Saint more relevant to our time, or any time?

In Chapter V, "Thérèse's Faith — and Ours," Fr. Connor concentrates on one of the greatest needs of our times. It's a very consoling chapter, as he demonstrates how few people in the course of the Church's life have clung to their faith so tenaciously amidst such a variety of circumstances as Thérèse did. Every event of the young Saint's life speaks to our own. If in her humanness she learned to strengthen her faith through the happenings of her life, should anyone who follows the Lord really expect to do less!

In Chapter VI, Fr. Connor again emphasises Thérèse's relevance, she has much to say on prayer: It is an aspiration of our hearts, time spent with God, not our time but his. Using God's Word, spending time in his presence, and doing it over and over again, never tiring, never letting go.

In Chapter VII, "Thérèse and Suffering," Thérèse says much with which to console us: "Let us profit from one moment of suffering. Let us see only one moment. A moment is a treasure. One act of love will make us know Jesus better, it will bring us closer to Him during the whole of eternity."

Chapter VIII, "A Saint for the Pessimist." The pessimist in each of us makes us read this chapter avidly. What Thérèse offers is a true spiritual optimism — true, because it is so realistically grounded. Her many words written in Story of a Soul and elsewhere, are not merely the outpourings of a great Saint with no meaning for us. Fr. Connor brings this out very strongly. Thérèse wrote with us in mind — with every little soul in the world in mind, excluding only those who were too spiritually advanced.

Chapter IX deals with the Holy Eucharist and the priesthood. Thérèse reminds us that it is not to remain in a golden ciborium that Jesus comes in the Eucharist, but to nourish, strengthen and console us.

No writing on Thérèse would be complete without reference to her love for the Blessed Virgin (Chapter X). Thérèse's deep devotion to Mary began perhaps with the loss of her mother at 4 years of age and the subsequent loss to Carmel of her two older sisters, Pauline and Marie. Perhaps this is why she cultivated a deep devotion to the Mother of God at an early age and it was such an important component of her spiritual life. Fr. Connor observes that the uniqueness of her contribution to Mary in devotion was her emphasis on Our Lady as a mother more than a queen.

The final chapter, "The Church's Doctor for the Third Millennium," sees Thérèse in all her glory, in all her relevance to the Church of the third millennium. In the case of the Church's newest Doctor, the more one studies her the more one is called to rediscover a theology made on the knees, which not only nourishes the mind, but satisfies the whole being, helps it to find its inner unity… hers is the reality of an intense mystical life in daily life, in the present moment, always in contact with what is basic to daily human existence.

Fr. Connor, I believe, has made an invaluable contribution to understanding our beloved Thérèse in the most intimate way. I hope this wonderful book gets the widest circulation in the English-speaking world. Not only that, but I equally hope it will be quickly translated into all the other principal languages. He has given to us what Pope John Paul II described in his Apostolic Letter on St. Thérèse, *The Science of Divine Love*: "The core of her message is actually the mystery itself of God-Love, of the Triune God, infinitely perfect in Himself. If genuine Christian spiritual experience should conform to the revealed truths in which God communicates Himself and the mystery of His Will (cf. *Dei Verbum*, n. 2), it must be said that Thérèse experienced divine revelation, going so far as to contemplate the fundamental truths of our faith united in the mystery of Trinitarian life. At the summit, as the source and goal, is the merciful love of the three Divine Persons, as she expresses it, especially in her *Act of Oblation to Merciful Love*. At the root, on the subject's part, is the experience of being the Father's adoptive children in Jesus; this is the most authentic meaning of spiritual childhood, that is, the experience of divine filiation, under the movement of the Holy Spirit. At the root again, and standing before us, is our neighbor, others, for whose salvation we must collaborate with and in Jesus, with the same merciful love as His."

Fr. J. Linus Ryan, O. Carm.
Director of St. Thérèse National Office
Carmelite Community
Terenure College
Dublin 6W, Ireland

Feast of St. Thérèse 2006

INTRODUCTION

Throughout the centuries, great sages have debated the meaning of human life, the destiny of man, and what love means. Left on its own, the human race has come up with a number of replies. Some answers have indeed been wise. Other responses have unfortunately proven quite destructive. What ultimately comforts us is that we have NOT been left alone. Our heavenly Father has sent His Word and Son, Jesus Christ, to give us the correct answers to the above questions. Christ's Church, ever enlightened by the Holy Spirit, "the Spirit of Truth," continues to instruct us how to live in love and holiness here on earth. Indeed through His Church, Jesus assures us that holiness and authentic love practiced during our earthly lives will not end in oblivion, but in eternal life in heaven. Members of the Church, armed with such consoling truth, know precisely what is the meaning of life.

In recent decades, the word "love" has not always been used in a truthful way. Even those great saints whose lives of love we admire too often have their teachings about love redefined to suit current worldly thinking. One needs only to think of what the modern world has done with the loving heritage of Saint Francis of Assisi to understand this assertion. How have we gone from the authentic "Il Poverello" of Assisi, who loved Jesus to the point of sharing His sacred Wounds, to the bland statue we see in the garden fountain? Saint Francis' example of love has been reduced to something solely emotional, an arbitrary sentiment. The real Francis was seized by God's condescending merciful love. He was in awe over the fact that God should take on our human flesh in order to save us. Saint Francis simply spilled over in wonderment at God's mercy. He understood that authentic love is the love shown to us by Jesus on the Cross. Only to the extent that we live a similar love can we call ourselves authentic followers of Christ.

Among those disciples of Christ who have understood the authentic nature of love, a debate has often ensued about what is more important: God's love for us, or our duty to respond in love. In the seventeenth century, this debate was typified by the polar opposites of Jansenism and Quietism. The former emphasized to an extreme measure what we should do for God. The latter taught that we should let God do everything, as if God did not want our cooperation with His grace. These extremes, both condemned by the Church, are not peculiar to the seventeenth century. They can be found in one form or another throughout the Church's history. It seems fair to say that we can find them in circulation even today.

It is important that we be constantly vigilant about witnessing to authentic Christian love. We must persistently assert that true love is not confined to the emotions but involves our minds and wills, as our Holy Father, Pope Benedict XVI, has reminded us in his recent encyclical *Deus caritas est*. Furthermore, we must retain the authentic Catholic teaching that true love involves first God's merciful love for us, then our graced response to Him. Both movements are essential.

Father Charles Connor has immeasurably contributed to

a proper understanding of authentic Christian love by his present volume on Saint Thérèse of Lisieux. The Little Flower, like
Saint Francis, can be subject to misunderstanding. Her doctrine
on Christian love can be unduly tailored to suit current tastes.
Saint Thérèse was someone who was awed by God's love for her,
but she knew that this love involves the Via Crucis. She may
have avoided extreme penances to show her love for God, but she
probably suffered more in imitation of her Savior by consistently
loving God in the present moment, with THIS person, in THIS
situation. Saint Thérèse did not believe only in God's love for
her (and everyone else), but she understood deeply Jesus' command that we express this love in our daily lives, especially in a
missionary manner. The Church has rightfully proclaimed Saint
Thérèse as a Patroness of the Church's missionary activity. It is
not only loving deeds and even heroic measures which will make
Christ's Church grow, but above all prayerful solidarity with God
and with one another. After all, is it not this very prayerfulness
and love which helped the Early Church to grow, long before the
age of martyrdom?

The times in which we live seem particularly perilous. We
need to understand the authentic nature of love for God and man
more than ever. I am very grateful to Father Connor for instructing
us so clearly about what Saint Thérèse would have us learn about
love. Saint Thérèse's writings are not that voluminous, and they
have been examined by many authors and from many different
perspectives. Father Connor's thematic approach will prove help-
ful especially for the beginner, who has not yet read, or even heard
of *The Story of a Soul*. Indeed, it would be very surprising if many
more copies of Saint Thérèse's original writings are not examined
as a consequence of reading Father Connor's analysis of the Little

Flower's spiritual teachings. But even those of us who have immersed ourselves many times in Saint Thérèse's writings will be inspired once again by her, thanks to Father Connor.

Most Rev. Joseph F. Martino, D.D., Hist. E.D.
Bishop of Scranton
November 30, 2006

THE SAINT FOR THE THIRD MILLENNIUM:
THÉRÈSE OF LISIEUX

CHAPTER ONE

THE WORLD OF SAINT THÉRÈSE

Some years ago, Bishop Patrick V. Ahern, Auxiliary Bishop of New York, and a leading expert on the life and thought of Saint Thérèse of Lisieux, was making a retreat with a fellow New York Archdiocesan priest in the Catskill Mountains of New York State. One afternoon, he decided to take a somewhat lengthy walk to the nearest village, and as he walked down the steep hill leading into town, he noticed the steeple of the local parish church. He felt drawn to the solace presented by this particular setting, and went in to make a visit. While praying in the presence of Our Lord in the Blessed Sacrament, a strong spiritual insight hit him, compelling enough to jot down, lest he forget any of its particulars. All he found in the back of the church was the stub of a much worn pencil and a copy of the parish bulletin, but in the space he had, the Holy Spirit provided him this marvelous insight:

> There is need of a daily effort to live in the present moment, to accept myself constantly with all my flaws and all my sins — no matter what I am or feel I am just now, knowing that God who never changes, accepts and loves me.[1]

---

[1] Patrick V. Ahern, *Thérèse: An Intimate Companion* (New York: Alba House Cassettes, 1989).

With that brief thought, the Bishop captured, in captivating style, one of, if not *the* most crucial element, in the doctrine of Thérèse, the Saint he had studied and loved since student days at Saint Joseph's Seminary in Yonkers. Curiously, as he left the church that day, he realized he did not know the name of its patron. Turning around to glimpse any possible identification, he caught sight of the inscription over the front door: Saint Thérèse of Lisieux.

Thérèse's teaching on the merciful love of God, so present in Bishop Ahern's insight, is critical to an understanding of this "democrat of mysticism," who makes sanctity accessible to us all. The more one meditates on the writings of the Saint of the "Little Way," the more appealing and challenging her doctrine appears. She is appealing because she offers a simple, direct route to God; she is demanding because her simple, direct route stretches every fiber of our being. She was a woman of her time, and is a woman of our time because her world and ours are strikingly similar, separated by slightly more than a century, and filled with the on-going similarities of human nature. Writing on the centenary of her death, Professor Barry Ulanov of Barnard College, Columbia University, notes that

> She makes it possible for us, when we come to know her well, to put up with and to survive our world, and does so as the great moderns do, with an extraordinary... tough-mindedness. Hers, like theirs, is a realism that we may not yet, one hundred years later, fully understand or appreciate.[2]

---

[2] Barry Ulanov, "*Thérèse and the Modern Temperament*," cited in John Sullivan (ed.) *Experiencing Saint Thérèse Today* (Washington, DC: ICS Publications, 1998), 158.

This becomes all the more true when one examines her writings and how they demonstrate a significant knowledge of world events, political issues both in and out of her native France, and the topics columnists were writing about in French newspapers. As one Thérèse scholar has noted, if we, a century later, hope to "put on" the mind of the Saint of Lisieux, to understand how her thoughts developed, to see the world as she saw it, we must "tap into" that huge category we call "background" or "context."[3] We are all shaped or molded, to some extent, by the world in which we live, and Thérèse was no exception. To understand the woman she was, and the saint she would become, it is necessary to look at her world, the French Province of Normandy in the nineteenth century, a culture largely formed by the events of the French Revolution a century earlier.

The Revolution of 1789 did not simply happen. In many ways, it owed its origins to an earlier revolution in philosophical thought called the Enlightenment. The traditional thinking French Catholic of the late eighteenth century would have associated the movement with rationalistic thought, Deism and the like, and from such currents, political disorder and anarchy could logically follow. In this sense, the French Revolution was really part of a larger movement referred to by some historians as an Atlantic Revolution, a social unrest sweeping the Western world. Because France was the largest Catholic country, with the greatest number of monastic houses, as well as a nation which had produced a significant number of theological and spiritual writers, it could be argued that France was the center of an earthquake that changed the position of the entire Church.

---

[3] Leopold Glueckert, *"The World of Thérèse: France, Church and State in the Late Nineteenth Century,"* cited in Ibid., 10.

Much of the nation's financial resources had been expended in numerous wars fought over the decades, though French nobility and clergy had large sums of money because of their tax exempt status. The monarch began pushing the concept of tax reform to get more revenue from the large estates, but the nobility resisted, and the King was forced to convoke the Estates General, the highest representative body in the country, consisting of the nobility, clergy and freemen, or craftsmen who owned their own businesses. The fourth estate — the common people — were excluded. At one time, the Estates General had been convoked regularly to get their opinions and input, but as their power began to grow, succeeding Kings were less and less interested in convoking the body. In 1789, it was simple pragmatism — the government needed revenue — which prompted the emergency session.

Various classes were invited to draw up petitions for reform — both political and Church reforms were asked for, and significantly, many of the French clergy were asking the King, rather than the Pope, for reforms. Initially, there was no suggestion that anyone wanted the demolition of the Church or the monarchy; reform was all that was sought, especially reform of the monasteries, so that they might become places of useful work and contemplation. When the Estates General met, the clergy were very sympathetic with those people favoring serious reform. The nobility, on the other hand, wanted all three estates to vote separately on all issues, since the system was one which clearly favored the upper classes. Those of the third estate wanted the representatives of all three estates to form one representative assembly with each member having one vote. In this argument, the clergy (because so many of them were, by popular expression, lower clergy) took the part of the third estate, and thus played a decisive role in breaking the power of the nobility, and ushering in what became the French Revolution.

In 1790, the third estate withdrew from the Estates General and formed the new Constitutive Assembly with the lower clergy. This assembly soon took drastic reform measures, enacting them in a relatively short period of time so as to calm the unrest and quell much of the rioting on the streets of Paris. The clergy had to renounce their financial privileges; they became dependent on the state, received stipends from the government, and were reduced to the status of civil servants. The Constitutive Assembly then drew up the Civil Constitution of the Clergy, which reorganized diocesan boundaries to be coterminous with civil structures. This reduced the episcopacy by one-third: fifty-seven dioceses were suppressed and fewer parishes existed. Bishops and priests were to be elected by the civil electorate, and papal approval was unnecessary. The Pope ceased to have any authority in the French Church, and the French clergy were forced to take an oath of allegiance to this new Civil Constitution. All of this had a very serious effect on religious communities, including the order Saint Thérèse ultimately joined.

> ...[T]he Carmelites, as a religious family, were wiped out during the Revolution. This means that eight provinces of the ancient observance were eliminated; and there were another six provinces of the Discalced friars destroyed. This translates into 130 houses of the Ancient Observance with 721 friars.... The Discalced lost seventy-nine houses of friars and sixty-five monasteries of cloistered nuns. Some of the Discalced religious managed to maintain their identity long enough to re-found a house here or there, but for the Ancient

Observance, the suppression was permanent.... Some
of these re-foundations took place because the religious simply went underground to survive. Some
communities, in effect, never really died out even
though their houses were gone. In both branches of
the Order, there were priests or brothers or sisters who
managed to maintain connections with one another.
They lived a genuine "catacomb" existence until it was
finally safe to reemerge after the political storms had
blown over. But such success did not happen all that
quickly or all that often.[4]

By March, 1791, over fifty percent of the lower clergy had
taken the Oath of Allegiance to the Civil Constitution, while
many others (émigrés) went into exile — many coming to the
newly formed diocese of Baltimore, Maryland. Pope Pius VI made
clear his disapproval of the Civil Constitution, but his words were
not taken very seriously by the "eldest daughter of the Church."
In fact, the Church in France was now two: the Constitutional
Church (the only legal one), in which all sacraments were recorded; and the Roman Church. In the summer of 1791, King
Louis XVI tried to flee, and openly denounced the work of the
Revolutionary Government. He called on Prussia and Austria to
help restore his former position, but it was to little avail; he was
imprisoned the following year, and executed in January, 1793.

At this point, the monarchy was formally abolished and the
Republic — very revolutionary in its character — was established.
The National Convention, comprised of much of the fourth estate, became the ruling body, and launched a campaign against

---

[4] Ibid., 15.

the Church. Marriage was made a purely civil contract, and the Church had no say in it. The Cathedral of Notre Dame was dedicated to the goddess of reason, and all churches and chapels in Paris were to be closed. The Convention also drew up a new calendar with national holidays corresponding to the great events of the Revolution. Persecution of priests became commonplace, and many, under pressure, abdicated.

A period of moderation followed with the Directory — persecutions lessened, but the situation of the church was still not comfortable. Priests could only use churches with special permission and at limited times, and the celebration of the Mass was permitted only if it was done quietly. Also, the Constitutional Church received no financing from the French government.

In 1800, Pius VII assumed the papacy for what would be a twenty-three year reign. Less hostile to revolutionary ideals, he once declared there was no conflict between democracy and the gospel. He introduced a series of modernizing reforms in the papacy, and made it clear he wanted to maintain his independence from any temporal power. Some political conservatives thought him a dangerous radical, but it allowed him a chance to negotiate with the French government. Napoleon Bonaparte had recently concluded a successful coup d'état, establishing the Consulate and declaring himself First Consul. For pragmatic reasons, and no other, he initially declared himself favorable to reconciliation with the Church.

He was quick to secure freedoms for the Church, liberty of action for French clergy, and he insisted that French-occupied territories in the Papal States (over which the Pope was still temporal ruler) be free. Pius VII also seemed anxious for reconciliation, though the Holy Father and his Secretary of State, Cardinal Consalvi, proved much more unyielding on Church rights and privileges than Napoleon had expected. Though Church/state negotiations took considerably longer than initially thought, a Concordat was signed on July 15, 1801. Catholicism was recognized as the religion of the majority of the French people. It was to be exercised openly and freely, but the Church was to be subject to some police regulation where the government felt necessary. Problems existed with material possessions which had been confiscated and sold by the French government; properties not sold were left to the state — on this, Napoleon would not budge. Another difficulty was the existence of the Constitutional Church and the Roman Church in France. It was decided that all bishops in France should resign so that a new episcopate could be established. The new bishops would be nominated by Napoleon and named by the Pope, though the Pope could refuse these candidates if he felt them not worthy. Parish priests were to be nominated by the bishops, and the government had to approve them. Cathedrals and churches were to be given back to the clergy, and bishops and clergy would receive a salary from the state.

In April, 1802, Napoleon published this Concordat alongside another proclamation called the Organic Articles. He did this with no prior contact with Rome, his intention being to regulate the Church in France. What he gave away in the Concordat, he took back in the Organic Articles. The Articles stated that no communication from the Pope was to be published in France without the consent of the government; no papal representative would be admitted without the consent of the government; no seminary could be opened without Napoleon's personal consent, and the First Consul had to approve the governing rules of any such; seminary professors could only teach if they adhered to Gallican (French national) principles. Also, there was to be only one catechism and one liturgy for all of France; some articles were inserted in the catechism claiming Napoleon to be the new Charlemagne, and civil marriages were to precede church marriages.

Napoleon was proclaimed Emperor of the French in April, 1804, and he wanted the Pope to come to Paris to give him his blessing. Pius VII hesitated for three months, but finally accepted the invitation to come to the crowning. Fearing to appear too favorable to France, and possibly affronting other European nations, Pius nonetheless felt advantages outweighed disadvantages, and perhaps his presence might even contribute to mitigating the Organic Articles.

There is a famous portrait of Napoleon crowning himself Emperor with the Pope merely looking on. The Holy Father's visit to Paris boosted the morale of the people, supported French bishops and priests, and strengthened the religious fervor of the Catholic populace. It did nothing to change the Organic Articles. Many young people began to see the Pope in a different light. No longer a strange and distant figure, affection for the person of the Holy Father and strong French devotion to the papacy are clearly traceable to this visit.

Napoleon's policy of surrounding and enclosing the Papal States by regions led to the final rupture between the French government and the Holy See. In addition, as part of his famous Continental System, Napoleon asked the Pope if he would prohibit British vessels from coming into ports in the Papal States. Pius, wanting to maintain strict neutrality, refused. In 1808, Rome was occupied by French troops and the following year, Napoleon incorporated the Eternal City into the French empire. The Pope responded by issuing a bull of excommunication "to all who had perpetrated such actions." Pius was, in turn, arrested, transported to an Italian coastal town, and held in captivity. The Holy Father responded with a sort of passive resistance — he refused to invest any French bishops who had been nominated by Napoleon. Increasingly, French clergy and laity began to show resistance to Napoleon and, pragmatist that he was, he realized the time had come to negotiate with the Church.

In 1812, the Emperor arranged to have the Pope removed to Fontainebleau, and for six days the two leaders talked. They ultimately signed a provisional, confidential agreement in which the Pope consented to invest the new French bishops, but Napoleon — not keeping his part of the accord — went ahead and published the results of their negotiations as the Concordat of Fontainebleau. Pius responded with a formal retraction, which Napoleon chose to ignore. Napoleon's behavior toward the Church had filled the Catholic consciousness with indignation, and toward the end of the Napoleonic regime there developed a secret organization, the Chevaliers de la Foi, desiring to restore the Bourbon monarchy, as well as the temporal power of the Pope. They contended the faith was in danger as long as the principles of government were based on revolution.

In 1814, Napoleon was exiled to the island of Elba, returned for a brief hundred days, only to go into permanent exile. In the aftermath of these events, the papacy gained considerably. Of more significance nationally was the fact that after 1814, French Catholics became more politically conservative, very counter-revolutionary in thought. They began to see in the French Revolution and its aftermath, the work of the Devil, and they denounced any new tendencies that smacked of revolutionary rhetoric. They believed that wherever the Revolution had been successful, the Church had suffered; most came to feel there had been a fundamental contradiction between Catholicism and the ideals of the revolutionaries. By 1815, and the rewriting of the map of Europe at the Congress of Vienna, a certain religious revival was strengthening the Church. Many turned away from modern ideas of progress, and back to the traditional roots of Catholic philosophy of the Middle Ages. This was even felt in Protestant circles, with significant conversions to the Catholic faith throughout Western Europe. In a very special way, the French Church would be cast into this mold for well over a century, until the aftermath of the First World War:

> Although it had been shorn of much of its land and wealth, the Restoration church was much more spiritual and zealous, better disciplined, and far more conscious of Gospel values than its predecessor. Most of the old prince bishops had either died off, or been replaced, or had simply resigned and fled to save themselves. By the end of the nineteenth century, Catholics had regained their confidence and political power, especially in the more conservative provinces, such as Thérèse's Normandy…. It was not until the time of the Third Republic, the time of Thérèse, that we begin to see the first glimmers of a new and conciliatory attitude: that maybe a strong, healthy, free-standing church could live within a republic…. Maybe the mission efforts of the church would work after all… even alongside republican institutions.[5]

Some twenty-three years after the Restoration, in 1838, the Carmelite Monastery of Lisieux was established on the Rue de Liverot. It was founded by nuns from the much older Carmel at Poitiers, and, like many other foundations of the time, probably

---

[5] Ibid., 20.

had not gone through the legal formalities of being re-established by the government. By 1880, when Thérèse was a young girl, and the thought of a religious vocation had surely entered her mind, there were one hundred thirteen monasteries of Discalced Carmelite nuns in France.

Religious life in the Little Flower's homeland had, therefore, gone through much travail since the French Revolution, but in those struggles there was a real strengthening and a new vibrancy. Those entering foundations like Carmel in the final two decades of the nineteenth century would know the historical background, and be strengthened in their own resolve by the example of older religious who had endured so much.

Saint Thérèse's own life began in 1873, the same year as the singer Enrico Caruso, and Sergei Rachmaninoff, the Russian pianist and composer. Emperor Napoleon III died in exile that year, and the last of the German armies were leaving France after a very difficult period of occupation following the Franco-Prussian War. Pope Pius IX had been reigning for nearly a quarter century, and would continue for five more years. If religious life in France had been strengthened by the hardships of the eighteenth century, the spiritual life of the Church was similarly enhanced by this Pontiff who consecrated the entire Catholic world to the Sacred Heart of Jesus, solemnly defined the doctrine of the Immaculate Conception of the Blessed Virgin Mary, and presided over the First Vatican Council, which is perhaps best remembered for its constitution, *Pastor Aeternus*, declaring papal pronouncements on matters of faith and morals infallible, not because of the consent of the Church, but by the guidance of the Holy Spirit given the successor of Peter when he speaks "ex cathedra." Professor Alan Schreck has aptly noted that:

Whatever criticism is made of Pius IX's attitude toward the modern world must be seen in light of the great renewal of Catholic faith and life that resulted from his policies. This century was not only an age of challenges, but also of reawakening of the Catholic faith, led not only by Popes, but by great saints as well.[6]

In 1887, after he had been Pope some nine years, Pius' successor, Leo XIII, would meet one of those great saints, when a young girl of fourteen begged him, during the course of an audience, to grant her permission to enter Carmel at the age of fifteen. As she was hurried out of the room after the Pope had given her a few kindly words, he never realized a Saint had been in his midst.

Without compromising Catholic truth for one moment, Leo tried to reach a rapprochement between Catholicism and modern culture. His fear was the Church in the modern age would come to be seen as a foreign, hostile power, and he was anxious to enter into dialogue with many of the constitutional governments springing up around the world. He attempted this in Thérèse's native France; in England, he made John Henry Newman, the famed convert, a Cardinal, much to the delight of his fellow countrymen. Likewise, he made the theology of Saint Thomas Aquinas normative for judging all Catholic philosophy and theology. He opened the Vatican archives to scholars and researchers, and encouraged them to use new approaches, all the while reaffirming the value of traditional Catholic theology, and stressing the need to guard against modern errors.

---

[6] Alan Schreck, *The Compact History of the Catholic Church* (Ann Arbor, MI: Servant Books, 1987), 98.

The final quarter of the nineteenth century is best understood by events preceding it, the way in which the Church responded to them, and the society which emerged as a result. Saint Thérèse of Lisieux would live the twenty-four years of her earthly life in this final quarter century, and bequeathed to the Church a spiritual legacy entitling her to be called the Saint for the Third Millennium. Looking at the world in which she lived, prepares us to examine more closely the person she was.

CHAPTER TWO

WHO WAS THÉRÈSE MARTIN?

Saint Leonard's Bridge in the Norman town of Alençon remains largely unchanged from its appearance in the late 1850's. Zélie Guerin, a young woman of the town, was once crossing the bridge and saw a young man walking on the opposite side.

[His] distinguished appearance, dignified bearing, and reserved manner struck her. At the same moment, an interior voice murmured, "This is he whom I have prepared for you." His identity was soon revealed to her, and she came to know him more intimately.[1]

The young man was Louis Martin, and the two were married on July 15, 1858, at the Church of Notre Dame in the center of Alençon. They would become the parents whom Saint Thérèse of Lisieux described as "more worthy of heaven than of earth." Louis Martin was born in Bordeaux in 1823, the son of a military father whose career necessitated the family move from one city to another. His wife Zélie, eight years younger, born in Gandelain, was also of a military family. Both had felt called to religious vocations as children; Louis had had a very difficult time mastering

---

[1] Stéphane-Joseph Piat, OFM, *The Story of a Family* (Rockford, IL: TAN Books and Publishers, Inc., 1994), 40.

Latin, so essential to priestly studies, while Zélie was strongly discouraged by a religious superior to whom she had confided her soul. Each was to follow a different course in life, and follow it well. Louis mastered the intricate art of watch and clock-making, and served a long apprenticeship before opening his own business. Zélie would become expert at lace-making, for which Alençon was famous. Of the two families, the Guerins seemed to have played a far greater role in the life of Saint Thérèse. Zélie's sister, Marie Louise, would enter the Visitation Order at LeMans, and become known as Sister Marie Dosithee; her brother, Isidore Guerin, was a pharmacist, and one of the leading Catholic laymen of Lisieux.

Because of an intensely religious background, Louis Martin, at the time of his marriage to Zélie Guerin, suggested they live celibately, as brother and sister. After nine months, a confessor told them they were not to continue, but were to be husband and wife. Thank God for the wisdom of that confessor; it allowed them to become the parents of nine children. Of the nine, four died in infancy,[2] and of the five who lived, Marie, born in 1860, became Sister Marie of the Sacred Heart in the Lisieux Carmel; Pauline, born in 1861, became Mother Agnes of Jesus, and served twice as Prioress of the same Carmel, her second term, for life, in deference to her sainted sister; Leonie, born in 1863, had many emotional difficulties in her life, and tried religious life with the Carmelites, the Poor Clares, and finally entered the Visitation Order at Caen, where she spent many fruitful years[3]; Thérèse would enter Carmel on April 9, 1888, and be followed six years later by

---

[2] Hélène: October 13, 1864-February 22, 1870; Joseph-Louis: September 20, 1866-February 14, 1867; Joseph-Jean-Baptiste: December 19, 1867-August 24, 1868; Mélanie-Thérèse: August 16, 1870-October 8, 1870.

[3] For the most thorough treatment of Leonie, see Marie Baudouin-Croix, Leonie Martin: A Difficult Life (Dublin: Veritas Publications, 1993).

her older sister Céline (born in 1869), who would be known as Sister Genevieve of the Holy Face. The four Martin sisters were joined in the Lisieux Carmel by their first cousin, Marie Guerin, daughter of Isidore Guerin, who took the name Sister Marie of the Eucharist. In fact, there were five members of the same family in this monastery, totally at variance with the thinking of the Carmelite reformer Saint Teresa of Avila, who favored no more than three. An exception was made in this case, however, because of the truly remarkable nature of this family.

Thérèse was the ninth of nine children, born January 2, 1873, in Alençon, where her eight siblings had also been born. She has often been described as belonging to the bourgeois, the mercantile or middle class of French society, reflected somewhat by the Rue Saint Blaise on which she was born, a street

> ...named from an ancient devotion in Alençon to the glorious martyr. An historical mansion attracts the traveler's attention. Approached through a royal court of honor, it is a remarkable example of the style of Louis XIII, the Hotel de la Prefecture, which once sheltered the piety and alms deeds of a spiritual daughter of the Abbé de Rance, the Duchess of Guise, before serving as the residence of the royal commissioners and subsequently of the administrators of the department. Just opposite, at no. 42 — formerly 36 — a stone tablet points out to the pilgrim the house in which Thérèse of the Child Jesus was born. It is modest and inconspicuous in its red brick; the front room on the ground floor is lighted by two windows provided by exterior shutters; the first floor, pierced by three French windows provided by exterior shutters; the first floor,

pierced by three French windows with elegant fan-lights, opens to a balcony, the iron railing of which runs the entire length of the house front, and a single dormer window on the roof lights the topmost room. Formerly detached on its right hand, and separated by a railing from the neighboring buildings, on its left it joined a building as quiet as itself.[4]

Thérèse would live in this house the first four and one-half years of her life, excepting a period from March 1873 until April 2, 1874, when, because of the poor health of her own mother, she was brought to Semalle, to the home of Rose Taillé, a wet nurse. Feeding problems would be far from the worst difficulty Zélie Martin faced — in just a few short years, breast cancer would claim her life. While she had her health, and the family was united in one household, it was an extraordinarily happy one.

> God was pleased to surround me with love, and the first memories I have are stamped with smiles and the most tender caresses.[5]

One peculiar incident occurred when Thérèse was no more than four years old. Her sister Leonie, thinking she was too old to be playing with dolls, showed her a chest filled with fine dresses, and materials for making more. She jokingly offered them to little Thérèse, who enthusiastically responded "I choose all!" The memory would remain with her.

4   Piat, op. cit., 118-119.
5   John Clarke, OCD (trans.), *Story of a Soul: The Autobiography of Saint Thérèse of Lisieux* (Washington, DC: ICS Publications, 1996), 17.

This little incident of my childhood is a summary of my whole life; later on, when perfection was set before me, I understood that to become a saint, one had to suffer much, seek out always the most perfect thing to do, and forget self. I understood too there were many degrees of perfection — each soul was free to respond to the advances of Our Lord — to do little or much for Him; in a word, to choose among the sacrifices He was asking. Then, as in the days of my childhood, I cried out "My God, I choose all."[6]

Some time after Zélie Martin's diagnosis, a pilgrimage to Lourdes was planned with her three eldest daughters. While there, she took the baths four times each day, her daughters asking her each time if she had been cured. In fact, she was in terrible agony, but upon her return first to LeMans (where her sister was stationed), and later to Alençon, where she had to face many of the skeptical, she said many times she had no regrets about making the pilgrimage, and all was in God's hands. Zélie seemed much resigned to her fate, perhaps the greatest miracle she could have hoped for. She continued her work both as mother and lace maker until she no longer had strength, and her death came in November, 1877.

The memory of her mother's death would leave an indelible impression on Thérèse, despite her young age. The room in which she died (the same room in which Thérèse had been born) is adjacent to a second floor chapel today, and one may still see the site of these events. Her father brought her to her mother's casket to kiss her goodbye, and of this farewell, the Saint later wrote:

---

[6]   Ibid., 27.

I did not speak to anyone about the deep feelings I experienced — I looked and listened in silence.... Once I was standing in front of the coffin lid; I stood looking at it for a long time. I had never seen one before, but I knew what it was. I was so little that, in spite of Mama's small stature, I had to lift up my head to see the top of it, and it seemed to me to be so big, so dismal.[7]

At the age of four and a half, Thérèse experienced the hard realism that everyone must experience in the course of life, and difficult as it was for a child of her age, it would serve her well in her own spiritual journey. The day of her mother's funeral was to prove decisive for her future life.

After the religious ceremonies in the Church of Notre Dame the family returned home plunged in sorrow. "The whole five of us," says Thérèse, "stood together in a group mutely gazing at one another in our grief. The maid seeing us thus was moved to compassion, and, turning to Céline and myself, she exclaimed: 'Poor little children, you have no longer a mother.' Then Céline, throwing herself into Marie's arms cried: 'It is you who will be Mama for us now.' And I, accustomed as I was to follow Céline in everything, would also have imitated this action, so beautifully appropriate, but I thought that Pauline would perhaps feel sorrowful and forsaken, having no little daughter. I looked up at her

---

[7] Cited in Guy Gaucher, OCD, *The Story of a Life* (New York: HarperCollins, 1993), 26.

tenderly, and leaning my little head on her heart, I said: 'As for me, Pauline will be my Mamma'."[8]

By her own admission, Saint Thérèse divides her life into three periods: the first, from her birth until the death of her mother; the second, from age four and a half until her famous "conversion" on Christmas Eve, 1886 (the most difficult period), and the final stage, from that conversion through her religious life in Carmel. The first period ended with the family's departure from Alençon less than three months after the death of her mother. Louis Martin was now fifty-four years of age, with five daughters to raise, and all the attendant difficulties facing any father in such a situation. As such, he seemed only too happy to take the advice of his brother-in-law, Isidore Guerin, and resettle his family in Lisieux, also in Normandy, and today, no more than a two-hour train ride from Alençon. Thérèse was not to visit the site of her birth again for six years.

Les Buissonnets has become well known to Lisieux pilgrims, and devotees of Thérèse everywhere. It was the name given their new home by the Martin children, and is located close to the center of the town, on the Deauville-Trouville Road. In Thérèse's time, it would have been heavily traveled by tourists en route to French beaches. By nineteenth century standards, it surely was a residence for upper middle class, and the Saint of Lisieux would live there until she entered Carmel in 1888. For the Martin family, their new town was a somewhat different environment.

---

[8] Cited in Msgr. August Laveille, *Life of the Little Flower: Saint Thérèse of Lisieux* (New York: McMullen Books, Inc., 1953), 61.

With its 18,600 inhabitants, linen thread and cloth mills, cider presses, tanneries and distilleries, Lisieux could claim to be the principal industrial city of Calvados. The Saturday markets filled the town with produce from the Norman countryside. Lisieux still looked medieval with its old streets lined with half-timbered houses; the rue aux Fèvres (Street of Fevers); rue du Paradis, rue d'Ouville, place des Boucheries (Butcher's place). On feast days the military band of the 119th Infantry regiment made a cheerful noise in the public gardens in the shadow of the Cathedral.

After the 1870 war the town declined because of a recession in the textile industry. Several strikes broke out, and the birth rate fell. But the Martins lived on the fringes of that world.[9]

Marie and Pauline, the oldest girls, would tend to the daily maintenance of Les Buissonnets, while Thérèse, still so very young, was filled with youthful enthusiasm.

At Les Buissonnets my life was truly happy… the affection with which I was surrounded helped me to grow.

How sweet were the conversations we held each evening in the Belvedere! With enraptured gaze we beheld the white moon rising quietly behind the tall trees, the silvery rays it was casting upon sleeping nature, the bright stars twinkling in the deep skies, the light breath of the evening breeze making the snow

---

[9] Gaucher, op. cit., 32.

clouds float easily along; all this raised our souls to heaven, that beautiful heaven whose 'obverse side' alone we were able to contemplate.[10]

The conversations Thérèse describes were very often spiritual, further enhancing their family's happiness. Time spent with the father whom she loved reflects this even more:

Each afternoon I took a walk with Papa. We made our visit to the Blessed Sacrament together, going to a different church each day, and it was in this way we entered the Carmelite Chapel for the first time. Papa showed me the choir grill and told me that there were nuns behind it. I was far from thinking at the time that nine years later I would be in their midst![11]

Among the churches she mentions, two in particular stand out: the parish church of Saint-Jacques, and the Cathedral of Saint-Pierre. Saint-Jacques was the parish of the Martin family, and they would often attend Mass there on weekdays, though not on Sunday, because no pews were available in an era when families paid individual rents to occupy designated places in church. It was here, however, Thérèse's sister Pauline always said she found her Carmelite vocation. The Cathedral was just a short distance away, and here the Martins attended Sunday Mass, as well as Vespers on Sunday evenings. In 1888, Louis Martin donated the high altar in this Norman Gothic style structure, and it was here Thérèse made her first Confession. Years later, her recollections took her back to the Cathedral when she wrote:

---

[10] Christine Frost, *A Guide to the Normandy of St. Thérèse of Lisieux* (Birmingham and Dublin: The Thérèsian Trust and St. Thérèse Missionary League, 1994), 20.

[11] Ibid., 13.

All along the way to the church and even in the church Papa's little queen (Thérèse) held his hand. Her place was by his side, and when we had to go down into the body of the church to listen to the sermon, two chairs had to be found side by side.... Uncle, (Isidore Guerin) sitting in the wardens' pews, was always happy to see us come.[12]

At the age of eight and a half, Thérèse entered the Abbaye Notre Dame du Pré, a girls' school at the Benedictine Convent. She would remain there until she was thirteen, and she would describe these years as the unhappiest of her life. Perhaps the loss of her mother some years before, perhaps the scrupulosity she would begin to suffer as a child, perhaps the loss of her two sisters to the Lisieux Carmel, Pauline and later Marie, perhaps the attitude of some of her classmates who made fun of her, perhaps all these and more contributed to her overall malaise. Yet it was here she made her First Holy Communion and Confirmation, and where she returned for two afternoons a week in the Spring of 1887, in order to be received into the Association of the Children of Mary. These were also the years when a deep spiritual life was being rooted in her.

One day one of my teachers at the Abbey asked me what I did on my free afternoons when I was alone. I told her I went behind my bed in an empty space which was there, and that it was easy to close myself in with my bed curtain and that I thought. 'But what

---

[12] Ibid., 25-26.

do you think about?' she asked. I told her I thought about God, about life and about eternity.[13]

At age ten, two very significant events occurred in her life. The first was an unusual illness, described years later by her sister, Mother Agnes of Jesus, as one consisting of…

> attacks of terror with horrible visions and an urge to throw herself head-first off the bed. She said afterwards that she never lost the use of her reason for one moment, and that when she seemed to be unconscious she actually heard and understood everything that was being said around her. She was always convinced, too, that the devil had a lot to do with these phenomena. Whatever about that, the illness disappeared suddenly on 10 May, 1883, and never troubled her again.[14]

It was, she felt, the intercession of the famous "Virgin of the Smile," namely a statue of Our Lady of Victories present in her room, which brought about her cure. Many spiritual theologians are of the opinion that she did indeed witness an apparition. In the same year, she read a biography of Saint Joan of Arc, and was convinced that she, too, was called on to be a great saint.

> …I received a grace which I have always looked upon as one of the greatest of my life, because at that age I wasn't receiving the lights I am now receiving…. [God] made me understand my own glory would not be

[13] Ibid., 23.
[14] Christopher O'Mahoney (ed.), *Saint Thérèse of Lisieux by Those Who Knew Her* (Dublin: Veritas Publications, 1995), 62.

evident to the eyes of mortals; that it would consist in becoming a great saint...! I don't count on my merits, since I have none, but I trust in Him who is virtue and holiness.... God alone... will raise me to Himself and make me a saint, clothing me in His infinite merits.[15]

At age thirteen, the third period of her life began in which she put childhood and immaturity behind, gave up her overly sensitive nature, and, though she may not have known it, became one of the church's great spiritual masters. As always, on Christmas Eve, 1886, she and her family attended Midnight Mass in the Cathedral of Saint-Pierre. It was a long-standing tradition among the French to fill the children's stockings with gifts and place them over the fireplace. The Martins returned from Mass, and Thérèse went upstairs to hang up her coat and hat. As she was climbing the stairs, she overheard her father say, "Well, fortunately this will be the last year!" Her older sister, Céline, knowing her very sensitive nature, was sure she would burst out crying, and tried to persuade her not to go downstairs until she had regained her composure. At that moment, she received a great grace, went down to the living room with absolutely no sign of emotion or unhappiness, and thoroughly enjoyed the Christmas celebration with her father and sisters. It seemed the Christ Child's strength supplanted her weakness, the strong character she had as a small child of four and a half was restored to her, a ten-year struggle had ended, her tears had dried up. Freed at last from herself, she embarked on her race for sanctity. She began to forget herself, and to be concerned with others, and in so doing, she discovered true happiness.

---

[15] Clarke, op. cit., 72.

On that night of light began the third period of my life, the most beautiful, and the most filled with graces from heaven. The work I had been unable to do in ten years was done by Jesus in one instant, contenting Himself with my good will which was never lacking. I could say to Him like His apostles: "Master, I fished all night and caught nothing." More merciful to me than He was to His disciples, Jesus took the net Himself, cast it, and drew it in filled with fish. He made me a fisher of souls. I experienced a great desire to work for the conversion of sinners, a desire I hadn't felt so intensely before.[16]

Interestingly, the Holy Spirit was much at work in France that same Christmas Eve. A young man named Paul Claudel went into the Cathedral of Notre Dame in Paris a convinced atheist, and came out thoroughly transformed. He went on to become a significant author, Catholic apologist, and onetime French Ambassador to the United States. Vicomte Charles de Foucauld also wrote of the "first Christian Christmas" of his life, based on experiences of the same evening. Among other things, he would go on to found the Little Brothers of Jesus.

Another significant episode occurred in July, 1887, proving Thérèse had indeed come out of herself and had a mind for others, in fact, had an apostolic vocation. She was following the Mass from one of the side chapels in the Cathedral of Saint-Pierre, and as she closed her missal, a picture of the crucifixion slipped from its pages:

One Sunday, looking at a picture of Our Lord on the Cross, I was struck by the blood flowing from one of

---

[16] Ibid., 98-99.

the divine hands. I felt a great pang of sorrow when thinking that this blood was falling to the ground without anyone's hastening to gather it up. I was resolved to remain in spirit at the foot of the Cross and to receive the divine dew. I understood I was then to pour it out upon souls. The cry of Jesus on the Cross sounded continually in my heart: 'I thirst!' These words ignited within me an unknown and very living fire. I wanted to give my Beloved to drink and I felt myself consumed with a thirst for souls.[17]

Thérèse had to have been influenced in her own desire by the Carmelite vocations of Pauline and Marie. She was crushed when each left, since both, in their turn, had been mother to her. Thérèse visited them often in the parlor of Carmel, and was filled with all sort of emotion. At the same time, the spiritual hunger welling up in the young saint was entirely her own. It would be difficult to discern the moment her vocation crystallized, though she was quite clear she wished to enter the monastery on December 25, 1887, the first anniversary of her conversion. Strange as the modern temperament might consider this coming from a girl only fourteen, she was intensely resolute. At Les Buissonnets, in the back of the home, there is a striking marble depiction of Thérèse kneeling alongside her father, seeking his permission to enter Carmel. Louis Martin was of a mind to thank God that yet another of his daughters felt called to religious life. In the conversation he had with her, he referred to her as a "little flower," one who had been preserved in her fragility and obscurity. He told her of her sheltered, though by no means naive life, picked a small

---

[17] Frost, op. cit., 32.

white flower from the garden, and gave it to her. The roots came up with the stem when her father pulled it, and she took this as a sign she would be transplanted to Carmel. Later, when the stem broke, she saw a further omen that she was not to remain long on this earth.

The members of the Carmelite community, including the Prioress, Mother Marie de Gonzague, and Mother Genevieve, the saintly foundress of the monastery, were much in favor of Thérèse entering, but diocesan authorities were slower to express such enthusiasm. Exercising a very understandable concern because of the unusual nature of such a request, the chaplain of the Carmel, the Vicar General of the Diocese and the Bishop himself were all, in varying degrees, less than positive. Thérèse met with the Bishop of Bayeux, Msgr. Hugonin, and there is a famous picture of her, wearing her hair up in more mature style. It shows how strikingly beautiful a girl she was, and it was done for effect — she wanted to convey the impression of being older than fifteen, something which gave the Bishop much delight when he was told the story!

It sounds almost humorous to say if all else fails, take your request to the Pope, yet that was the mind of Thérèse when she accompanied her father and many other French pilgrims on a journey to the Eternal City to celebrate the golden sacerdotal jubilee of Pope Leo XIII in 1887. Under the leadership of Msgr. Germain, Bishop of Coutances, one hundred ninety-seven French pilgrims embarked on their journey on November 4th, and among their number were seventy-five priests. The pilgrims began at the magnificent church of Our Lady of Victories in Paris, where a stained glass window still depicts Thérèse and her father kneeling in prayer. The young saint was able to see the wonders of Paris, then on to Italy, where the group visited such cities as

Milan, Padua, Venice, and Bologna, before landing in Rome. Sunday, November 20th brought the long-awaited papal audience, at which the pilgrims were strictly instructed to kneel, kiss the ring of the Holy Father, and move along quickly. The story is well known of Thérèse forthrightly asking the Holy Father for permission to enter Carmel at the age of fifteen, his response to her to follow the will of her superiors, the annoyance of the Vicar General, who explained to the Pope that it was a matter that diocesan officials were looking into, Thérèse's further plea, if only the Holy Father would say yes, it would be a reality, his reply that if God willed it, it surely would be so, and her finally being escorted away. Curious that today Mass is offered in honor of Saint Thérèse of Lisieux, not in honor of Leo XIII, marvelous pontiff though he was!

One could only imagine the broken heart of the young girl. We catch a glimpse of it from a letter she wrote to her sister Pauline, Sister Agnes of Jesus, at the Lisieux Carmel the same day. Acknowledging the "good God" was making her pass through many trials before entering Carmel, she recounted the events of the audience to her sister, and then she added

> ...I cannot tell you what I felt, it was like annihilation, I felt deserted, and then I am so far, so far.... I could weep as I write this letter, my heart is so full. Still God cannot be giving me trials beyond my strength. He gave me the courage to sustain this one. Oh! It is a very great trial, but, Pauline, I am the child Jesus' little ball; if He likes to break His toy, He is free to; yes, I do indeed want what He wants.[18]

---

[18] Thérèse to Sister Agnes of Jesus, 20 November, 1887, cited in F.J. Sheed (trans.), *Collected Letters of Saint Thérèse of Lisieux* (New York: Sheed and Ward, 1949), 37.

The pilgrimage would continue until December 2nd, and there are many interesting particulars of Thérèse's life associated with it. Of great import are the lessons she took from her travels, most especially those about human nature. Souls must be prayed for, especially those consecrated to the good Lord.

There were two things the Little Flower learned during her pilgrimage — to disdain the world and to pray for priests. Up to that time, she said, the principal aim of Carmel was unknown to her, a mystery to her. She had seen the need to pray for sinners... because Jesus Christ came to take on Himself the sins of the world, to die for sinners, to lay down His life for His brothers. But for priests, those men who put on Christ, who stand for Christ in the eyes of the faithful and through whose anointed hands we receive the sacraments — those outward and visible signs of grace — that we should have to pray for them with the same heart and fervor with which we pray for sinners was hard for her to realize until she made this pilgrimage.[19]

Her acceptance into Carmel would not be long in coming. An official letter of permission from the Bishop arrived during the Christmas holidays, 1887, but the delay which followed was on the part of the monastery. It was felt that Thérèse's entry should be postponed until after the strict Lenten fast was completed. She lived with this very great disappointment, and finally achieved her goal on April 9, 1888. One may still see the door through which she entered the cloister and at which she knelt to receive

---

[19] Dorothy Day, *Thérèse* (Springfield, IL: Templegate Publishers, 1991), 122-123.

her father's blessing. She was entering a community of twenty-six religious, a monastery described as small and poor, soon to celebrate its fiftieth anniversary of foundation. The sisters who welcomed her into their midst were anything but strangers — they had known her since she was a child, and had seen her many times on her visitations to her sisters, and on other special occasions that would bring local townspeople to the Carmel. Bishop Guy Gaucher, Auxiliary Bishop of Bayeux and Lisieux, a great Thérèse scholar, and himself a Carmelite, situates the monastery's internal structure in 1888:

> The Carmelite life had been reformed in the sixteenth century by St. Teresa of Avila.... This exceptional woman, who was both a mystic and a very practical person, founded little "deserts" where enclosed religious sought God privately (two hours of mental prayer daily) and in communal prayer, while working in an atmosphere of friendship and joy. The Spanish foundress, full of common sense and with her feet on the ground, laid down a balanced way of life where love must take precedence over all, including the practices of mortification, which are only means. Three centuries later some Carmels had been diverted toward indiscreet ascetical practices, sometimes toward a narrow moralism. The Lisieux Carmel had not escaped these tendencies which the general climate of French Christianity — with its Jansenist leanings — encouraged. The spirit of penance and mortification was in danger of taking precedence over the dynamism of love. More than one Carmelite was terrified of God the judge.[20]

---

[20] Gaucher, op. cit., 88-89.

This was the atmosphere Thérèse encountered, and because of her young age, she was subject to more intense scrutiny than if she had been, say, twenty-one at the time of her entry. At least one of her biographers has gone to great pains to debunk the myth that she was severely persecuted, a common theme in older versions of her convent life. Thérèse herself gives a glimpse of Carmelite life in a letter to Céline, the last Martin sister to enter Carmel. One month after her acceptance she admitted there were moments

> …when I ask myself can it be true that I am at Carmel; sometimes I can't believe it! Alas, what have I done for God that He should so fill me to overflowing with His graces? "…[W]hat does it matter whether life is cheerful or sad, either way we shall come to the end of our journey here below." A day passed by a Carmelite without suffering is a day lost.[21]

It was in this Carmel Thérèse spent the final nine years of her life, and gave the world her magnificent autobiography, *The Story of a Soul.* This was not a work she wrote from beginning to end; rather, it came about through an interesting set of circumstances. Thérèse had a wonderful recollection of childhood memories which she would often relate to the community. One evening at recreation, Sister Marie of the Sacred Heart told her younger sister she should write down these stories. Thérèse thought she was joking, but in a far more serious vein, she asked Mother Agnes of Jesus, who by now was Prioress, to put Thérèse under obedience to record her memoirs. In her spare time over the next several months, she did just that, and when completed,

---

[21] Thérèse to Céline, 8 May, 1888. Cited in Sheed, op. cit., 48-49.

gave them to Mother Agnes, who subsequently placed them in a desk drawer and did not read them for several months. Thérèse had such composure over her emotions; she never asked her sister her opinion of what she had written. These childhood reflections became known as Manuscript A. Sometime later, Marie again asked her sister to explain in greater detail this "Little Way" she was always speaking of. She answered Marie's query in a letter of about a dozen pages — this letter became Manuscript B, the heart of the autobiography. Finally, near the end of her young life, Mother Marie de Gonzague, who had come back into office as Prioress, asked her to record her convent memories. This final part of the autobiography, Manuscript C, was written during periods of tremendous pain and suffering, and by July, 1897, she had to cease writing altogether. Given such duress, the beauty of her very credible prose is all the more remarkable.

On Holy Thursday evening, April 3, 1896, Thérèse had no sooner gone to bed than she felt something like a stream come bubbling up to her lips. Since it was already dark, she waited until the next morning to examine her handkerchief and see that it had indeed been blood. She had a strong premonition this was the beginning of the end, and was overjoyed that her earthly life was slowly but surely coming to an end; that she would soon join her beloved in heaven. It would be another full year before the tuberculosis ravaging her body would really be felt. As the month of April, 1897 wore on, there was vomiting, acute chest pains and frequent coughing up of blood. By July, she was confined to the infirmary, and began to experience all the humiliations of any bedridden person: fevers, profuse sweating, suffocation, insomnia, constipation, bed sores, and gangrene of the intestines. This was coupled with intense moral suffering, what has been called her "night of nothingness." To read the many accounts of the last days of Thérèse is to be struck with a tortured soul totally consumed by love of God, and living to the full all she had written about and to others. She finally breathed her last, speaking the words, "My God, I love you," on September 30, 1897, coincidentally, the same day a young child was baptized in Italy named John Baptist Montini — he would become, some sixty-six years later, Pope Paul VI.

The usual obsequies followed, as they might for any deceased Carmelite, and young Sister Thérèse of the Child Jesus and the Holy Face was the first religious buried in the Carmelite plot that Uncle Isidore Guerin had donated in the town cemetery. As time would prove, it would not be her final resting place.

> The few mourners withdrew, convinced that the little Sister's earthly role was over. But, a few days later, a wooden cross was erected at the head of the grave. In addition to the name of Soeur Thérèse de l'Enfant Jesus, it bore these mysterious words: "Je Veux Passer Mon Ciel a Faire Du Bien Sur La Terre." This announcement, which was so promptly realized, was to make of this lowly mound, crowned with lilies and roses, a shrine of supplication and thanksgiving almost unparalleled in the whole world.[22]

One year to the date of her death, Thérèse's autobiography, *The Story of a Soul*, was published, carrying the Bishop's imprimatur and many corrections by Mother Agnes, who tried to render a work as much in keeping with her sister's thought as possible. In slightly more than fifteen years, the Lisieux Carmel had sent out over two

---

[22] Lavielle, op. cit., 320. "I want to spend my heaven in doing good on earth."

hundred thousand copies. As early as 1905, translations had been made into English, Polish, Italian, Dutch, German, Portuguese, Spanish, Japanese, and Russian. This "storm of glory" overwhelmed the Carmelite community at Lisieux and caused Sister Marie of the Eucharist (Marie Guerin) to write to a cousin:

> Everyone is speaking to us about this beloved angel who is doing so much good through her writings. Priests are comparing her to Saint Teresa and saying she has opened up a whole new way to souls, the way of love. They are all enthusiastic, not only around us, but throughout France, and in most of their sermons they are quoting from the inspired passages of her manuscript. There are even men in the world, whom piety somewhat embarrasses, who are enthusiastic about it and have made it their favorite reading.[23]

The practical manifestation of this "storm of glory" can be seen to this day around the walls of the chapel of the Lisieux Carmel. Crutches are found in abundance, and in the walls are individual blocks of concrete inscribed with various family names, and specific thanksgivings to Thérèse for favors granted through her intercession. No sooner had the twentieth century begun, than calls for her canonization began to be heard. The famous editor, Louis Veuillot, reported in his paper l'Univers, that initial steps in the process were beginning to be taken in Rome. In March, 1907, Pope Saint Pius X let his enthusiasm for her cause be known, when he made his oft-quoted statement that Thérèse was "the greatest Saint of modern times." He would not be the

---

[23] Sister Marie of the Eucharist to Céline Pottier, 12 February, 1899. Cited in Gaucher, op. cit., 209.

Pope to canonize her, though he had, in effect, canonized her by his words. The diocesan beatification process began in the summer of 1910, and that fall her body was exhumed in the presence of several hundred persons; her remains were then transferred to another vault.

The apostolic process began in Bayeux on Saint Patrick's Day, 1915, was somewhat slowed down by the intervention of the First World War, but brought to a conclusion, after ninety-one sessions, at the end of October of the same year. Pope Benedict XV exempted the cause from the usual fifty-year waiting period, and promulgated the decree on the heroic quality of her virtues in 1921. Benedict was succeeded by Pius XI, a truly Thérèsian Pope who made her the "star of his pontificate," and kept her picture on his desk at all times, praying to her before he made any important decision. It was he who beatified her in 1923, and canonized her in 1925, before some fifty thousand persons. Pius would send Dennis Cardinal Dougherty of Philadelphia as his personal legate to Lisieux for the official ceremonies following her canonization, and two years later, he proclaimed her "Principal Patroness of the Universal Missions with Saint Francis Xavier." This was a curious, and very significant combination: a young girl saint who never left her cloister in a small town in Normandy, placed on equal footing with a Spanish Basque Jesuit who traveled extensive portions of the then known world. The Holy Father was stating quite clearly that the spiritual apostolate of prayer is surely as efficacious as the physical presence of missionaries in foreign lands.

As the years went by, it was soon discovered by students, biographers and devotees of Thérèse, that there was an "embarrassment of riches" with which to get to know her all the more. Her older sister Céline (Sister Genevieve of the Holy Face) was an apt photographer, and upon her entry to Carmel, Mother

Agnes of Jesus allowed her to bring her camera into the cloister, and she has given us many original photographs, both of Thérèse alone, and with the community. From them, we catch a glimpse of Carmelite life. In addition to her magnum opus, *The Story of a Soul*, much written record survives, and Pope John Paul II, in his Apostolic Letter proclaiming Thérèse a Doctor of the Universal Church, sums up the extant sources:

> In the 266 Letters we possess, addressed to family members, women religious and missionary "brothers," Thérèse shares her wisdom, developing a teaching that is actually a profound exercise in the spiritual direction of souls. Her writings also include 54 poems, some of which have great theological and spiritual depth, inspired by Sacred Scripture. Worthy of special mention are *Vivre d'Amour!...* (Poésies 17) and *Pourquoi je t'aime, ô Marie!* (Poésies 54), an original synthesis of the Virgin Mary's journey according to the gospel. To this literary production should be added eight "Recreations pieuses": poetic and theatrical compositions, conceived and performed by the Saint for her community on certain feast days, in accordance with the tradition of Carmel. Among those writings should be mentioned a series of 21 Prayers. Nor can we forget the texts of all she said during the last month of her life. These sayings, of which there are several editions, known as the Novissima Verba, have also been given the title *Derniers Entretiens*.[24]

---

[24] Pope John Paul II, *Thérèse of Lisieux: Doctor of the Universal Church* (Strasbourg: Editions du Signe, 1997), 18.

All of these sources have nourished the spiritual lives of millions in the century plus since her death. For the first fifty years, she was almost exclusively the Little Flower, a sentimental, though powerfully attractive figure for millions. In 1945, the emphasis began to change somewhat. Father André Combes, a professor of history of Spirituality at the Institut Catholique in Paris, and a medievalist by training, decided to devote his lectures that year to a study of Thérèse of Lisieux. At least one of his colleagues is said to have thought him mad! Nonetheless, the lectures were eventually published as *The Spirituality of Saint Thérèse (An Introduction)*. It introduced an entirely new direction in Thérèsian studies, but did not enjoy wide circulation until the centenary of the saint's birth in 1973.

In anticipation of the conferral of her doctorate, an International Thérèsian Congress was held at the Carmelite White Abbey in Kildare Town, Ireland, in the summer of 1997. Cardinal Cathal Daly, former Archbishop of Armagh and Primate of all Ireland, delivered one of the papers. The Cardinal very carefully traced the evolution in approach to the person and writings of Thérèse, and felt that the earlier devotional style may well have emerged in response to Mother Agnes' initial corrections, if not rewriting of her sister's words.

> …she was a product of her time and was conscious of a readership which had certain preconceptions about what was fitting for a saint, which it might have been unwise to disturb too radically. *The Story of a Soul*, in its original version, had provided spiritual nourishment for a whole generation of people across the world, and was certainly responsible for a multitude of vocations

to religious life and a multitude of conversions and of lay vocations of holiness.[25]

None of which, according to the Cardinal was bad:

> Styles of iconography and vocabularies of devotion are time-conditioned; they date quickly, and they often become insufferable to the next generation. But the reality which they, however inadequately, symbolized, the faith and the life which they once nourished, these are changeless.[26]

At the time Cardinal Daly delivered this paper, nearly a quarter century had elapsed since the centenary of Thérèse's birth. In those years, the Cardinal saw the real Thérèse emerging, coming more sharply into focus. This newer, and according to him, more authentic Thérèse, calls forth a new type of holiness in the church, more closely aligned, one might think, with the New Evangelization called for by John Paul II.

Thérèse promised her autobiography would contain something for everyone, except those who felt themselves too spiritually advanced. Through her immense appeal, she has more than proven her prediction of spending her heaven doing good on earth, and she has forever put to rest the worry two members of her community expressed to one another about the necrology of the saint following her death. "What will we ever find to say about Thérèse?" one sister fretted to the other. "She never did anything!"

---

[25] Cardinal Cathal B. Daly, *Thérèse: A Saint for all Seasons* (Kildare Town: Thérèsian International Congress, 1997, Unpublished Paper).

[26] Ibid.

CHAPTER THREE

THE "LITTLE WAY" OF CONFIDENCE AND LOVE

In October, 1895, Mother Agnes of Jesus received a letter from a young missionary priest, Father Maurice Bellière. His purpose in writing was twofold: he was in need of a spiritual confidant to whom he could pour out his soul; he was also in need of continuous prayer, for himself, his priesthood, and the missionary vocation he felt God was calling him to. Bellière felt one of the community of the Lisieux Carmel could fill this role, and he asked the Prioress if a specific sister might be assigned his correspondent. Mother Agnes asked her younger sister, Thérèse, if she would take on the task, and she was overjoyed. Thérèse had always yearned for a brother, especially a priestly one. She had been deprived of her own two brothers who died in infancy; she felt one of them might possibly have filled that void in her life. Now, with the request of Father Bellière, her prayer seemed to have been answered.

A series of twenty-one letters were exchanged between Maurice and Thérèse, and within less than a year of their initial correspondence, a strong spiritual bond developed. Thérèse had begun by addressing Maurice as "Monsieur L'Abbé"; by April, 1897, she referred to him as "my dear little brother." As they poured out their souls to one another, Thérèse could easily tell

Bellière was a deeply troubled soul. In one missive, she described much of herself, and told him of her great admiration for Joan of Arc. In studying the history of her country, Joan's exploits had greatly impressed her, and she felt called to a similar heroism, though far removed from the public view. In the silence of the Lisieux Carmel, she was being called to spiritual heroism, to be a great saint, to do for others what is the lot of all saints, making Christ lovable. Then, as if fearing she had created a mistaken notion in Father Bellière's mind, she described her true self:

> My dear little Brother, I must tell you that there was one thing in your letter which saddened me. It is that you don't know me as I am in reality. It is true that to find great souls one must come to Carmel. Just as in virgin forests flowers grow which have a fragrance and beauty unknown to the world, so Jesus in His mercy has willed that among these flowers there should grow smaller ones. I can never be grateful enough to Him, for it is thanks to that condescension that I find myself, a poor flower without distinction, on the same level as the roses who are my sisters. O my Brother! I beg you to believe me that the good God has given you as your sister not a *Great* soul, but one who is *Very Little* and very imperfect.
>
> Don't think that this is humility which prevents me from recognizing the gifts of the good God. I know that He has done great things in me and every day I sing to Him for doing so. I remember that the one who has had much forgiven is obliged to love more. Moreover, I try to make my life an act of love, and I no longer worry about being a *Little* soul. On the contrary,

I rejoice in this. This is why I dare to hope "my exile will be brief," but this is not because I am *Ready*. I feel that I shall never be ready unless the Lord Himself sees fit to transform me. He can do it in an instant. After all the graces with which He has filled me, I still await that of His infinite mercy.[1]

She was teaching the young priest a very important lesson, one that she did not arrive at easily or quickly; weakness is not a liability in approaching God, it is an asset. We can approach God no matter how poor we are, no matter how weak we are — in fact, our liabilities are actually our strengths, because they show us how total and complete our reliance on God must be. When Thérèse developed these thoughts for Maurice, she was developing something very novel — what has been properly called a "Copernican revolution" in spirituality — namely, no matter what situation we find ourselves in, the only criteria is that we place our trust in His merciful love.

Before we can fully appreciate her "little way," we must consider her thoughts on God's merciful love. Her sense of this was very vivid, and she felt that God's love was much like a flood tide longing to envelop humanity. At the same time, she was keenly aware of what a rejection of His love on the part of humanity meant to Him. In fact, she clearly saw that God's love was spurned on every side, much reminiscent of the words of John the Evangelist, that Our Lord had come unto His own, and they had not received Him. In June, 1895, on Trinity Sunday, Thérèse was attending the community Mass, and an inspiration came over

---

[1] Thérèse of the Child Jesus and of the Holy Face, Rel. Carm. Ind. to Maurice Bellière April 25, 1897, cited in Patrick V. Ahern, *Maurice and Thérèse: The Story of a Love* (New York: Doubleday, 1998), 104-105.

her with tremendous force — she must make a victimal oblation of her life to the merciful love of God. She took very seriously the words of the Lord that all who would come after Him, if they would be His disciples, must take up their crosses and follow Him. She realized that all who are baptized into Christ, who was both priest and victim, are called not only to share His priesthood, but also His victimhood, to be with Him on the cross throughout their earthly lives. When Pope Pius XI canonized her in 1925, he underscored this theme, teaching the entire Catholic world — and beyond — that this very novel approach was open to all, and he made his own, Thérèse's prayer of supplication in which she beseeched the Lord to cast His glance on a "legion of little victims" so worthy of His love.

On the Tuesday following Trinity Sunday, in company with her sister Céline, she knelt before a statue of the Blessed Virgin — the Virgin of the Smile — and made this oblation:

> O my God! Most blessed Trinity, I desire to *Love* you and make you loved, to work for the glory of holy Church by saving souls on earth and liberating those suffering in Purgatory. I desire to accomplish your will perfectly and to reach the degree of glory you have prepared for me in your heavenly kingdom. I desire, in a word, to be a saint, but I feel my helplessness and I beg you, O my God, to be yourself my sanctity![2]

The way of confidence had been growing, and this was its most symbolic expression. In order to offer herself to merciful love, she had to go through a kenosis — a self-emptying — something

---

[2] Cited in Christopher O'Donnell, O.Carm., *Love in the Heart of the Church* (Dublin: Veritas, 1997), 38.

every soul in the world must go through if it is to find God's love. This process is the only way to discover our littleness, which is by no means weakness, but rather the heart of the gospel message and a request the Lord makes of us all. Thérèse was actually initiating her "little way," and proving the truth of one theologian's comment decades later, that her entire system was "derived straight from the Gospels as God had interpreted them for her."[3]

In September, 1896, Thérèse began a private ten-day retreat, the last one she would make on this earth. Prior to this, she had been speaking with her sister Marie, who had been disconcerted with her lack of spiritual growth, and curious to discover more about the "little way" her younger sister had been speaking of. In an attempt to answer her sister's inquiries, Thérèse wrote Marie a letter during the course of the retreat, describing its components. In addition, she also composed a "letter to Jesus." Both these letters comprise Manuscript B of *The Story of a Soul*. Some days after the retreat's conclusion, she wrote a further letter to Marie that did not become part of the Manuscript, but nonetheless contains a very clear description of the "little way."

> ...to love Jesus, to be His victim of love, the weaker one is, without desires or virtues, the more apt one is for the operations of that consuming and transforming love.... It is trust and nothing but trust that must bring us to love.[4]

[3] Hans Urs von Balthasar, *Thérèse of Lisieux: The Story of a Mission* (London: Sheed and Ward, 1953), 168.

[4] Thérèse to Sister Marie of the Sacred Heart, 17 September, 1896, cited in F.J. Sheed (trans.), *Collected Letters of Saint Thérèse of Lisieux* (New York: Sheed and Ward, 1949), 289-290.

How do we achieve this littleness by which we may confidently come to God? Thérèse would give three practical steps: prayer, Scripture, and the sacraments, especially the Holy Eucharist. These are what enable us to lose ourselves in Christ, and give to others a spirit of charity, quite distinct from the weaknesses human nature often manifests. Practically, Thérèse is speaking of taking the very ordinary events of daily life, and making them our means of sanctification. In her autobiography, she gives a practical example from her own community experience.

> There is in the Community a sister who has the faculty of displeasing me in everything, in her ways, her words, her character, everything seems very disagreeable to me. And still, she is a holy religious who must be very pleasing to God. Not wishing to give in to the normal antipathy I was experiencing, I told myself that charity must not consist in feelings but in works; then I set myself to doing for this Sister what I would do for the person I loved the most. Each time I met her I prayed to God for her, offering Him all her virtues and merits. I felt this was pleasing to Jesus, for there is no artist who doesn't love to receive praise for his works, and Jesus, the Artist of souls, is happy when we don't stop at the exterior, but, penetrating into the inner sanctuary where He chooses to dwell, we admire its beauty. I wasn't content simply with praying very much for this Sister who gave me so many struggles, but I took care to render her all the services possible, and when I was tempted to answer her back in a disagreeable manner, I was content with giving her my most friendly smile, and with changing the subject of the conversation....

Frequently when I was at recreation (I mean during the work periods) and had occasion to work with this Sister, I used to run away like a deserter whenever my struggles became too violent. As she was absolutely un-aware of my feelings for her, never did she suspect the motives for my conduct and she remained convinced that her character was very pleasing to me. One day at recreation she asked in almost these words "Would you tell me, Sister Thérèse of the Child Jesus, what attracts you so much toward me; every time you look at me I see you smile?" Ah! What attracted me was Jesus hidden in the depths of her soul; Jesus who makes sweet what is most bitter.[5]

This very practical approach to spirituality has a strong biblical foundation. Some decades ago, the Swiss theologian, and later Cardinal Hans Urs von Balthasar studied her doctrine from this point of view, and concluded that her mission was similar to that of Saint Paul the Apostle. Thérèse places herself at the center of the gospel message, he feels, by "demolishing the religion of works for the sake of pure love." Our Old Testament forebears believed that their works justified them, that God's justice was appeased by the righteous acts of an entire life. The more righteous one's conduct was, the more positive accomplish-ments one achieved, and the more one could hope for salvation. Von Balthasar notes that this attitude overlooks what Saint Paul considered the "raison d'être of God's testament with the chosen people," namely the faith of their father Abraham, based not

---

[5] John Clarke, OCD (trans.), *Story of a Soul: The Autobiography of St. Thérèse of Lisieux*, (Washington, DC: ICS Publications, 1996), 222-223.

solely on fear of God's justice, but also on love. The Jewish people forgot that their good works merely pointed to the coming of the Messiah and the fulfillment of the law He would bring. It was very easy to attribute undue significance to the law as a means of justification, thinking of God merely as a God of justice, and not as a God of love. Von Balthasar makes the point that God wished to prepare humanity for love by means of the law, but He also wished "the failure of the law and its works to demonstrate what happens when men rely upon their own achievements apart from the Cross of Christ."[6]

At this point, Thérèse inserts what he calls her "New Testament theology," following closely on Saint Paul's teaching, so clearly expressed to the early Christians of Rome:

> Now, if a man does a piece of work, his wages are not "counted" as a favor; they are paid as debt. But if without any work to his credit he simply puts his faith in him who acquits the guilty, then his faith is indeed "counted as righteousness."[7]

This text must be joined with another, also from Romans:

> For all alike have sinned, and are deprived of the divine splendor, and all are justified by God's free grace alone, through his act of liberation in the person of Christ Jesus.[8]

Thérèse, says von Balthasar, follows Pauline teaching exactly: "In the evening of this life I shall appear before you

---

6 Von Balthasar, op. cit., 187.
7 Romans 5:4-6.
8 Romans 3:23-25.

empty-handed for I do not ask you, Lord, to count my works.... I want to be clad in your own justice, and receive from your Love the possession of Yourself."[9] Having made the transition into a New Testament, Pauline approach, Thérèse develops her unique school of thought:

> The "little way" that Thérèse now constructs comes from renouncing everything in Christian love which seems to lend it greatness, power and glory. Love is brought to a state of weakness in which it learns the power of divine love, of littleness and darkness in which the greatness and glory of divine love are displayed. The basis of the "little way," therefore, is one series of renunciations after another.[10]

Thérèse herself explained the little way as one of spiritual childhood, a way of trust and total surrender, a mindset which recognizes one's nothingness and total dependency on God, much as a child is totally dependent on his father. It is a way of holiness to which we must give our all, surrender our selfishness, our egotism, our greed, etc., and give without counting the cost. It calls for the practice of the virtues at every opportunity, and the realization that after we have done all we can do, we are still those unprofitable servants of whom Scripture speaks — servants totally dependent on their Master and His merciful love. It is the most optimistic way to sanctity because it never allows of discouragement, and it is a "little" way; little because it bypasses extraordinary methods, little because it presupposes the everyday, mundane lot of all humans as its sphere of activity, and little in that it is open to all. As Bishop

---

[9] Von Balthasar, op. cit., 189.
[10] Ibid., 199.

Patrick Ahern so beautifully expresses it:

> The Little Way is a whole new way of life, a way of holiness that is open to all because it requires nothing from anyone but the ordinary, day-to-day experience of which every life is made. Steeped in her mission of love, Thérèse saw no reason to take upon herself great penances, which were common in the Carmel of her day. She soon gave them up, content to offer God the small sacrifices which came in the routine of community life, the little occasions to be kind to others, the apostolate of the smile when smiling at another was the last thing she felt like doing. Such opportunities to demonstrate love for God by showing it to others abound in everyone's daily life.... The Little Way finds joy in the present moment, in being pleased to be the person you are, whoever you are. It is a school of self acceptance, which goes beyond accepting who you are, to wanting to be who you are. It is a way of coming to terms with life not as it might be but as it is.... The Little Way is a theology, one which is lived and one which rests on the rock foundation of a central divine truth: that God is nothing but mercy and love and can be counted on for His boundless benevolence.[11]

In Thérèse's own life, she discovered her vocation to be love in the heart of the Church. She expressed this in her Offering to Merciful Love, and would carry it out by means of her little way of confidence and love.[12] Father Conrad De Meester, a Belgian Carmelite and Thérèse scholar, has suggested the Little

---

[11] Ahern, op. cit., 114-115.
[12] O'Donnell, op. cit., 53.

Way be looked at on both a static and dynamic plane. Statically, it consists of a realistic assessment of our human weakness and sinfulness, all the while expressing confidence in God's merciful love. Dynamically, it is a daily progression in this attitude, what Thérèse herself described as becoming more and more little.[13]

In 1912, Francis Cardinal Bourne, then Archbishop of Westminster, made an oft-quoted confession of his own love for Thérèse because "she has simplified things: in our relationship with God she has done away with the mathematics."[14] The Cardinal echoed the feelings of millions of devotees of the Little Way, persons of all ages, nationalities, and walks of life who have taken Thérèse at her word, and adopted her approach to sanctity.

At the canonization in 1925, Pope Pius XI asked rhetorically, if the Little Way were seriously adopted, who could not see the reformation of society resulting? Years later, Dorothy Day, founder of the Catholic Worker Movement, and converted from a life of atheistic Communism to the Catholic faith largely through the influence of Thérèse, expressed her belief in a similar transformation. Just before the liberation of Paris in May, 1944, Pope Pius XII proclaimed Thérèse the "second patroness of France" along with Joan of Arc. Angelo Roncalli, the future John XXIII, once served as Papal Nuncio to France, and had the daily custom of praying before her statue in the chapel of the Nunciature in Paris, commending to her intercession, all the French people. Pope John Paul II became the first reigning Pope to go on pilgrimage to Lisieux, and to remind all present of the hunger of the human heart for God, and the childlike simplicity needed to reach Him.

---

[13] Conrad De Meester, OCD, *The Power of Confidence* (New York: Alba House, 1998), 15.

[14] Guy Gaucher, OCD, *The Story of a Life* (San Francisco: HarperCollins, 1987), 219.

Popes were not the only ones attracted to Thérèse. There was a remarkable young Jewish woman in Germany, trained in the philosophy of phenomenology, who converted to Catholicism, became, like Thérèse, a Carmelite, and ultimately lost her life in a Nazi death camp because of her Jewish heritage. In the world, she was known as Edith Stein, in religion, Sister Teresa Benedicta of the Cross. After reading Thérèse's *Story of a Soul*, she was filled with admiration.

> My impression was that this was a life that had been absolutely transformed by the love of God, down to the last detail. I simply can't imagine anything greater. I would like to see this attitude incorporated as much as possible into my own life and the lives of those who are dear to me.[15]

Saint Maximilian Kolbe, a Polish Franciscan who died in the same concentration camp as Edith Stein, had a deep love and devotion to Thérèse. Georges Bernanos, the renowned French author of *The Diary of a Country Priest*, had a similar devotion, and in speaking of Thérèse, observed that the world seemed to be dying because it had lost its sense of childhood. François Mauriac, one of France's leading Catholic authors, influenced by her writings, noted that it is never too late to become a saint. Charles Maurras, founder of Action Française, admitted in 1952, that he owed a great debt of gratitude to Thérèse. She had been his "good angel," and he always kept with him *The Story of a Soul*, as well as her relic, a personal gift from Mother Agnes.

---

[15] Waltraud Herbstrith, OCD, *Edith Stein: A Biography* (San Francisco: Ignatius Press, 1992), 123-124.

The Little Way is anything but an escape into childhood, a running away from the reality of life. As the observations of so many learned and holy people attest, it is an acknowledgment that eternal life is not something we attain by our own merits. "[It] is the free gift of our Father who loves us," one Carmelite observed, "all we have to do is accept it with the trusting heart of a child."[16] Thérèse herself spoke of it in her autobiography, when she told the story of one of the sisters in the community who was trying to light a number of candles for a procession, but had no matches. Instead, the sister took her light from a small vigil light burning in front of a shrine, with only the slightest flicker left. She was able to get a light, and from that light she lit the candles of all the sisters in the community. From this, she concluded that it takes only the slightest spark to light up the entire world. This was the message of her Little Way, a message she delivered to all who worry they are not better than they are.

She, therefore, makes all of us pause and consider our own inadequacies, our own failures in our ongoing attempts to love and serve God, and she makes us realize God loves us in spite of ourselves, in spite of our weaknesses and sins. In fact, He turns our weaknesses into our very strengths — strengths to love Him more, and to love our brothers and sisters in His Mystical Body all the more, and in doing that, everything else somehow falls in line — every aspect of our spiritual, moral and devotional lives.

[16] Eugene McCaffrey, OCD, *Heart of Love: Saint Thérèse of Lisieux* (Dublin: Veritas, 1998), 35.

CHAPTER FOUR

THÉRÈSE'S VIEW OF THIS LIFE AND ETERNITY

As a young girl in French Normandy, Thérèse Martin planned out her entire life; she thought, reflected, judged, and chose her path calmly, with great serenity, and clarity of vision. To her, life in this quickly passing, transitory, artificial world must never be taken too seriously. What must be taken very seriously is our growth in holiness and love of God, a love we experience without end in heaven. Knowing that when she arrived on heaven's shore her work would just be beginning, Thérèse's entire orientation in this world was to grow in holiness and love of God. It is given to few of us to approach earthly life with such intensity of conviction, though the more we come to know her, the same view can be ours.

> If Thérèse Martin became a saint, it was, I think, in the first place because, grace building upon nature, she had from early childhood a clear idea of life in general, and of her own life in particular, and because from the first she determined to live in accordance with this idea. Her progress in virtue was but a progressive realization of her ideal.[1]

---

[1] Abbé André Combes, *The Spirituality of Saint Thérèse* (New York: P.J. Kenedy & Sons, 1950), 1.

This development was life long, but is clearly discernible in the year prior to her entry into Carmel, 1887-1888. A good deal of the young girl's thought developed with the help of her older sisters, especially Pauline. Mother Agnes had known for a long time of her sister's desire to enter religious life, and in her correspondence from Carmel, she was painstakingly realistic about all it entailed, reminding her younger sister that into every life come difficulties. Thérèse responded forthrightly, welcoming any and all trials that might come her way, seeing them as an excellent means of detachment from all that modern secularity offered. Detachment was a common theme in nineteenth century spirituality, the idea of separating oneself totally or in part from all that could interfere with one's love of God. Whatever station in life a person occupied, detachment had much to offer the soul's spiritual advancement. Thérèse knew that trials and difficulties in life are a given, and can be dealt with only by keeping our eyes squarely fixed on Christ the beloved, who loves us so very much. In this, she hearkens back to Saint Augustine's concept of our human restlessness finding peace only in God, and if peace of soul can be experienced in some small measure in this life, it is only to the extent that each person realizes there is a divine plan for his or her life.

> The human soul can be satisfied, but to reach satisfaction it must look beyond this world, and to taste here below some small interior peace, it must conform its activities to the will of another, i.e., God.[2]

As soon as she was able, Thérèse looked upon all of life as a loving relationship with God; trials, difficulties, etc., were His

---

[2] Ibid., 4.

will for us, and His personal invitation to us, no matter who we are or what we do, to draw close to Him.

One reason that relationship with God was so important to cultivate was that the world as we know it is quickly passing away. A lesson in Thérèse's life brought this home to her very clearly. When she was about five and a half, a year after her mother's death, shortly after the family had moved from Alençon to Lisieux, her sister Pauline began to introduce her to the liturgical life of the Church. To be taken to Mass, and Vespers in the evening, brought her great joy, but no sooner had the Lord's Day begun, than it ended. Since even the Lord's Day is transient, she began to see that this earth is merely a place of exile, and true wisdom is yearning for the eternal happiness of our true home. The God she was growing to love more and more was her only anchor; reflecting years later on this period of her life, one incident had significance.

> That evening, at the hour when the sun seems to sink into the broad expanse of waters, leaving behind it a trail of light, I went with Pauline to sit upon a lonely rock. For a long time I gazed at this pathway of gold. She told me it was like God's grace which illumines here below the path of faithful souls. Then I pictured my own soul as a tiny barque with graceful white sails, floating upon this golden stream, and I determined never to steer it out of the sight of Jesus, so that it could sail swiftly and tranquilly towards the heavenly shore.[3]

This love of God became most pronounced in Thérèse's young life at age eleven, when she made her First Holy Commu-

---

[3] Cited in ibid., 8.

nion at the Benedictine School in Lisieux. By her own admission, these were unhappy years for her, though at this special moment of grace, she had the amazing foresight to see the world for what it truly was.

> A child of eleven, she was placed upon a summit, or rather upon the summit of human life. She had passed judgment on life, its dangers and its opportunities. Time was not enough; she needed eternity. At the age of fifteen she will have her wish; and soon after, heaven. It is the triumph of logical consistency, of sincerity, of humility, of the power of God.... She is literally sublime in her clear sightedness, her consistency, her prudence, her strength of will and her greatness.[4]

By the time she entered Carmel in April, 1888, she had accepted Christian teaching with absolute sincerity. As a religious, Scripture would increasingly nourish her, and she would build upon the foundation she received from *The Imitation of Christ* by Thomas à Kempis. Thérèse nourished herself on this spiritual classic from an age when most children would hardly have known what it was. As a result, she no longer accepts what is temporal, transitory, etc. as having any significant value; in one sense, she had already placed herself in eternal life at the beginning of her Carmelite vocation. One thought in a letter to her sister Céline fifteen months into religious life is very revealing.

> How hard it is to live on this earth! But tomorrow, in an hour, we shall reach the harbor. Then we shall see how wonderful is that life that has no end.... Our

---

[4] Ibid., 11.

Lord will be the soul of our soul. What an unfathomable mystery![5]

Her real citizenship was to be found in heaven, and she had no doubt someday she would assume her rightful place in the kingdom. This was not some sort of pie-in-the-sky dreaming, nor some Pollyannaish fancy. If it were, what possible explanation could be given to events occurring in her life on Good Friday, 1896?

The evening of Holy Thursday, April 2nd, Thérèse kept vigil in the choir until midnight. Scarcely had she gone to bed, when she felt a bubbling stream rising to her lips. Her lamp was extinguished so she did not try to find out whether or not it was indeed blood she had just vomited. She fell asleep. Upon rising, she partially opened the shutter and saw that her handkerchief was full of blood. What joy! She was deeply convinced that Jesus was inviting her, on the anniversary of His death, to come to Him. Thérèse informed her prioress and added: "I am not suffering, Mother, and I beg you to let me continue my observance of Lent to the end." Mother Marie de Gonzague did not realize the seriousness of the situation. She permitted Thérèse to work as if nothing had happened. She continued her fast and cleaned the windows of the cloister doors, standing on a stepladder in a drafty place. "The hope of going to heaven," Thérèse would write the following year, "carried me away with joy."[6]

---

[5]   Ibid., 19. See also: Thérèse to Céline, 14 July, 1889, cited in F.J. Sheed (trans.), *Collected Letters of Saint Thérèse of Lisieux* (New York: Sheed and Ward, 1949), 111-112.

[6]   Pierre Descouvement, *Thérèse and Lisieux* (Toronto: Novalis, 1996), 256.

This was the first manifestation of an excruciating illness that would claim her life, and it was coupled with intense spiritual torture. With such grim realities her daily lot, there was no time for the superficial. She knew very well what God was asking her to bear, the same kind of trials given to many who love much.

> Faced by the terrifying prospect of nothingness, Thérèse's faith stood firm. Just when she was deprived of all interior consolation, she wrote her most sublime pages on the love of God. Reduced to extremity, both physically and spiritually, she yet was able to show her love to all.... If she has become the gentle and sure guide for distressed souls, it is not due to any pretty fancies or cloying sweetness. She has won her victories at the point of the sword, or better, by the embrace of the cross. Her most grievous anguish of heart and soul was unflinchingly endured in the power of a love as sublime as the love of the greatest saints.[7]

It is because Thérèse is so very realistic, so attuned to the world, and so completely convincing in her view of life, that it would be difficult for anyone to ask: what could a young cloistered nun in a convent in Normandy in the nineteenth century teach me about a view of life, specifically the view I have of my life? She teaches, to all who are willing to listen, a detachment from things which are not important. She instructs us about a quickly passing world, very transitory for all of us, and about a relationship with God that must permeate every aspect of our being, as it did hers. The source of her strength, one Thérèse scholar has noted, was

---

[7] Combes, op. cit., 21-22.

the unchanging devotion of her love. That love was directed to the God she loved, and also to all whom God's Son had redeemed, her brothers and sisters in Christ's Mystical Body. If Thérèse had begun her heavenly life, in a certain sense on this earth, one of the reasons was her absolute conviction that the Church Triumphant in heaven, the Church Suffering anticipated love in purgatory, and the Church Militant on earth are intimately united. She expressed it well in verse:

> Heaven is quite close to earth
> The Lord knows your desires
> The Saints hear your prayer
> They gather up all your sighs
> The Blessed and the Holy Angels
> Ceaselessly protect you
> Of this all the Heavenly Host
> Have asked me to assure you.[8]

The term "Communion of Saints" has two closely linked meanings, a communion, or sharing in holy things, and among holy people. The *Catechism of the Catholic Church* is very clear who this is:

> …At the present time, some of His disciples are pilgrims on earth. Others have died and are being purified, still others are in glory, contemplating in full light God Himself, triune and one, exactly as He is…[9]

This is a beautiful definition of the Church, Our Lord the vine, and His members, the branches. The *Catechism* continues:

[8] Cited in Christopher O'Donnell, O.Carm., *Love in the Heart of the Church* (Dublin: Veritas, 1997), 55.
[9] *Catechism of the Catholic Church* (Liguori, MO: Liguori Publications, 1994), 249.

...So it is that the union of the wayfarers with the brethren who sleep in the peace of Christ is in no way interrupted, but on the contrary, according to the constant faith of the church, this union is reinforced by an exchange of spiritual goods...[10]

Shortly after giving this definition, the authors of the *Catechism* quote the young Saint of Lisieux in her desire to spend her heaven doing good on earth! The Church is, in effect, telling us Thérèse has something very important to teach us about the Communion of Saints.

Her relationship with eternity, and those who preceded her there seems to center on four areas. Our Blessed Mother (a study in itself), the saints, her own family, and her role once in heaven.[11]

Throughout her life, Thérèse found herself surrounded by many friends in heaven. The list of saints she mentions in her writings is very long, and some, like Joan of Arc, were beatified and canonized only after Thérèse herself. Also, once in the convent, and more immersed in Scripture, she developed a real love for many of the Old Testament figures. She does not appear to have composed, or for that matter recited lengthy prayers to any saint in particular, but, from time to time, she invokes a particular saint with exceptional fervor. Compared to the post-Vatican II Church, Thérèse placed a substantial emphasis on hagiography, and given the emphasis the *Catechism of the Catholic Church* places on the intercession of the saints for the Church in the twenty-first century, Thérèse appears prophetic.

---

[10] Ibid.
[11] Ibid.

Being more closely united to Christ, those who dwell in heaven fix the whole church more firmly in holiness. They do not cease to intercede with the Father for us, as they proffer the merits they acquired on earth through the one mediator between God and men. Christ Jesus... so by their fraternal concern is our weakness greatly helped...[12]

Thérèse's sense of the Communion of Saints, of our unity with those in heaven, was not restricted to canonized saints, but very much included her own family members. In Lisieux, the pilgrim gets a wonderful feel for this. Louis and Zelie Martin are buried on the hill which overlooks the magnificent basilica, erected years ago by Catholic devotees from around the world. In the town cemetery Thérèse's first resting place, are still to be found the graves of her siblings, to whom she had constant recourse throughout her life. When her mother died in 1877, she experienced her first loved one leaving her, but not really leaving her at all. Looking back on her First Holy Communion years later, she would write

...The absence of Mama didn't cause me any sorrow on the day of my first communion. Isn't heaven itself in my soul, and hadn't Mama taken her place there a long time ago? Thus, in receiving Jesus' visit, I received also Mama's. She blessed me and rejoiced in my happiness...[13]

Her relationship with her father was an especially close one, and the long illness he endured greatly tested her faith. Many

---

[12] Ibid.

[13] Cited in O'Donnell, op. cit., 63.

town gossips in Lisieux felt that Louis Martin's final illness was brought on by the devastation he felt when his youngest daughter had entered Carmel at the early age of fifteen. Nothing could have been further from the truth, but though she was now cloistered, the news of these stories reached Thérèse, and caused her tremendous sadness. Shortly after her father's death, she wrote what became a family poem:

> Remember that formerly on earth
> Your only happiness used to be to love us dearly
> Grant your children's prayer
> Protect us, deign to bless us still
> Up there you have again found our dear mother
> Who had gone before you into our holy homeland
> Now in heaven
> You both reign
> Watch over us.[14]

To her sister Leonie, an emotionally troubled soul who had tried religious life on four different occasions before finding stability, Thérèse continued in the same vein:

> …Do you not find, as I do, that our father's departure has brought us close to heaven? More than half the family now enjoys the vision of God, and the five exiled ones on earth will not be long in flying away to their homeland.… Are we not more united now that we gaze on the heavens to find there a father and a mother who offered us to Jesus?[15]

---

[14] Ibid., 62.
[15] Thérèse to Leonie, January, 1895, and 20 August, 1894. Cited in ibid., 62-63.

Thérèse saw her family as active members of the Communion of Saints, but also began to realize, as early as 1894, her own future role. She wrote to her sister Céline, who was still tending to their father…

> If I die before you, do not believe that I shall be far from your soul; never shall we have been more united.[16]

In March, 1897, just six months before her death, she made the Novena of Grace to Saint Francis Xavier, with the intention she would be able to accomplish much after her death. Writing to a second priest brother, Father Adolphe Roulland, she developed the idea with great clarity:

> When you receive this letter no doubt I shall have left this earth. Ah! Brother, I feel I shall be more useful to you in heaven than on earth, and it is with joy that I come to announce to you my coming entrance into that blessed city…. I really count on not remaining inactive in heaven. My desire is to work still for the church and souls.[17]

Her prediction was correct: she did not and does not remain inactive in heaven. Physical testimonies abound in the chapel of the Lisieux Carmel attesting to the gratitude of so many, and stories circulate through all parts of the world. In years past, these were often referred to as a "shower of roses," though one may apply any sort of term to God's answering prayer through the intercession of His saints. An early account of considerable note

---

[16] Thérèse to Céline, 23 February, 1896. Cited in ibid., 64.
[17] Thérèse to Adolph Roulland, 14 July, 1897. Cited in ibid., 66.

occurred less than fifteen years after Thérèse's death with the conversion to the Catholic faith of Mr. Alexander Grant, a former minister of the Free Church of Scotland. His wife had preceded him into the church, and the day after his baptism by a Scottish Jesuit, he and his wife left Edinburgh for Alençon, where, for many years, they were caretakers of the home in which Thérèse was born. Mr. Grant related the story of his conversion in detail to Mother Agnes, always attributing the grace which came to him to the young saint's intercession. Following Mr. Grant's death in 1917, his widow continued for many years to look after the Martin home, and to guide through its rooms the many pilgrims finding their way to Alençon. A significant number of conversions to Catholicism were noted in the years immediately following the saint's death throughout the largely Protestant British Isles. One woman's account is especially interesting:

> I belonged to a branch of the Anglican Church which was very near in doctrine to the Catholic Church. The infallibility of the Pope was the only Catholic dogma which seemed to me inadmissible. For six years I studied the arguments for and against that article of Faith, but I never could find more than a momentary satisfaction. Presently error would recover its sway and plunge me back into uncertainty. In the autumn of 1923, I bought a book called A *Little White Flower*. It made a profound impression on me. I felt near me the presence of Blessed Thérèse, and there grew up between us so close a friendship that we were really like two sisters. But, alas! There was one cloud that darkened my happiness — the soul of Thérèse and my soul were not united in faith. During the course of November I

asked the prayers of the Carmel of Lisieux, and received from them a relic of the Little Flower. I was delighted, and thinking our Anglican Vicar would be interested, I brought him my treasure. I shall never forget his scorn of my "superstition." I was extremely hurt, and conceived a strong aversion for the Anglican Church, whose teaching all at once seemed to me doubtful and capricious. "Is your faith dead, then?" said the Vicar, pointing to the relic. He spoke better than he knew. Where there was no place for Thérèse, there was no place for me, and since the religion of my birth rejected her, I, too, would be a Catholic.[18]

The woman in question, identifying herself only as "a grateful client," went on to describe how Thérèse completed the process of study, conversion and reception for her. On May 28, 1924, this very grateful woman was baptized Marie Thérèse.

Love of Thérèse in Ireland was based on many answers to prayers on the part of devout souls. In 1913, a jurist from County Donegal informed the Lisieux Carmel of the miraculous cure of his wife, who, shortly after the birth of one of their children was diagnosed with infectious septicemia, and given little hope of recovery. The family immediately began a Novena to the Little Flower, and the jurist reported one of his young daughters had received flowers from a mysterious Sister she had never seen — a sign, no doubt in their minds, that a cure was forthcoming. His wife did experience the answer to her prayers, and devotion to Thérèse was quick in spreading from County Donegal throughout the nation.

---

[18] Rev. Thomas N. Taylor, *Saint Thérèse of Lisieux, the Little Flower of Jesus* (New York: P.J. Kenedy & Sons, 1927), 393-394.

Still another story emerged from the Scottish village of Carfin, in the uplands of Lanarkshire. The town had mediaeval origins. Two ancient wells, in close proximity, were dedicated to Our Lady, and Celtic monks had come to spread learning. Irish and Lithuanian workers had eventually migrated there, all loyal to the Catholic faith. In later years, Roman monks had built churches and chapels in abundance, houses of worship that flourished until "the dark shadow of Calvinism settled upon the land; the monks were turned adrift, and only a few red embers were left of the great Eucharistic flames."[19] In 1920, five years before Thérèse was canonized, a grotto to honor Our Lady of Lourdes was constructed, and before long, a smaller, more modest shrine to the saintly Carmelite was built very close to that of the Blessed Virgin. A contemporary account takes up this curious story:

> ...On a memorable day it happened that the presence of the Little Flower was challenged, as if she were a rival that would rob the Immaculate Queen of her rightful glory. The challenge was submitted to her sisters in the Carmel of Lisieux, who, in indignation, promised that their Thérèse would accept it, and would prove her passionate loyalty to Mary by drawing a multitude of souls to the shrine. The promise passed into a prophecy, for in less than three months, a quarter of a million of pilgrims had wended their way to Our Lady of Carfin. Strange to say, the secular press vied with the Catholic papers in advertising her new sanctuary.[20]

---

[19] Ibid., 403.
[20] Ibid., 403-404.

This story had a sequel, whose effects were somewhat far-reaching. Carfin had been known for a splendid procession each year on the Feast of Corpus Christi. With the new influx of pilgrims coming to honor Our Blessed Mother and Thérèse, anti-Catholic hostilities were aroused, and forces of opposition succeeded in resurrecting an ancient penal enactment against carrying the Blessed Sacrament in public procession. Some years earlier, when a Eucharistic Congress was held in Westminster, this same legislation was successfully invoked, curtailing a certain amount of pageantry. In Carfin, however, the procession went on as planned, with no interference. The reaction against such hostility forced Parliament to have the long list of disgraceful enactments... "removed from the statute book of the realm."[21] In thanksgiving, the townspeople of Carfin erected a magnificent statue of Thérèse shortly after her canonization in May, 1925.

Abbot Godefroy-Madelaine was a member of the Premonstratensian Order, and Prior of a monastery in Calvados. He once gave a retreat at the Lisieux Carmel, and, in later years found himself Prior of another foundation in Frigolet. During the First World War, with the German occupation, he was forced to flee to an abbey in Belgium. In 1914, German troops ransacked the town, leaving little more than ruins.

> Hundreds from the neighboring population were imprisoned in the Abbey on August 23. At nine a.m. some sixty men were taken out and shot mercilessly. An hour later the Abbot was told the place would be set on fire. The religious — each of whom wore a relic of Saint Thérèse — begged earnestly that she would

---

[21] Ibid., 405.

aid them. At three o'clock they were threatened with execution, and two lay-brothers who tried to escape were murdered and flung into the [river] Meuse. It was a night of terror, for the town was burned to ashes, and they could hear the shouts of the drunken soldiery. Next morning a body of Saxons ransacked with great violence the entire convent, crying out that the monks were concealing soldiers and rifles. The Abbot and the Community were insulted and taken away... as prisoners.... [D]uring those weeks of detention they were at the point of death. Again and again when the danger was at its height it would melt away — no one knew how — but all felt that Saint Thérèse was with them. Finally, a Christian Brother, also interned, suggested a formal novena to the "little queen," and on the ninth day, September 24, General Berryer came to Marche, where they were imprisoned with the Carmelite Fathers, to announce their innocence and set them free.[22]

Desiré Cardinal Mercier (1851-1926), the internationally known Archbishop of Malines, Belgium, had a deep devotion to Thérèse. He believed that no one could read a work like Thérèse's autobiography without "the soul expanding and without experiencing more keenly the attractions of Divine Love."[23] Because of his closeness to the Little Flower, it is not surprising that he grew in friendship with the Lisieux Carmel, corresponding with them often, and leaving them his chalice after his death. At the end of 1925, he wrote to Mother Agnes, informing her he had been

---

[22] Ibid., 413-414.
[23] Ibid., 415.

diagnosed with serious cancer, and asking the entire community to beg Thérèse's intercession for whatever be God's will. In the brief six weeks remaining, the Cardinal kept her picture and relic with him continually, and on the day of his death, Mother Agnes received this note from the Archbishop's House in Malines:

> His Eminence has just left us to rejoin your little sister. It was the death of a Saint. If Thérèse did not obtain a miraculous cure, she has procured for him something better — a deathbed worth more than a long life. The last days were incomparably beautiful. And if she has not preserved him to us, she has done better. Our beloved Father is in Heaven — a source of grace and strength to his children. She has given us a Saint.[24]

Philadelphia's Cardinal Archbishop, Dennis Dougherty, was appointed by Pope Pius XI to be Papal Legate to Lisieux for the official ceremonies following Thérèse's canonization. Years earlier, he had been a Bishop in the Philippines, and encountered much hostility to the Church by Protestant missionaries, as well as much successful proselytizing by them of the native population. He wanted to build an orphanage and a hospital in his diocese, but to do so he would have to return home to raise funds, beginning with his native Archdiocese of Philadelphia. Dougherty had been a seminary professor and had never been engaged in parish work. He readily admitted that fund-raising was not his forte, but was resolved to do his best. While at home, he fulfilled a promise he made to a Carmelite nun in the Philippines to visit the Philadelphia Carmel. The sister who came to greet him was carrying,

---

[24] Ibid., 416.

quite by chance, a copy of *The Story of a Soul*, and asked the Bishop if he had ever read it. He replied he had not, nor was he familiar with who the Little Flower was. He began to read it, and very quickly developed a strong devotion to Thérèse. He entrusted the success of his campaign to her, and within a short period of time, had reached a sum of two hundred thousand dollars, no small amount in 1913. He made a pilgrimage of thanksgiving to the Carmel at Lisieux on his way back, and went ahead with his ambitious building project. The Cardinal traveled to many parts of the world; to Shanghai, to Tokyo, even to Arabia. In each of these places, he discovered copies of Thérèse's autobiography translated into the native language.

Volumes could be written describing Thérèse's activity in heaven — one story more interesting than the next. Some have claimed to have seen her, many have claimed the answer to prayers of petition, still others, sure guidance and direction. While the church is always the final arbiter of private visions, messages, revelations, and the like, the countless answers to prayers provide abundant evidence she is proving herself true. Thérèse promised to keep working until time is no more — what could possibly make any saint more relevant to our time or any time?

CHAPTER FIVE

THÉRÈSE'S FAITH — AND OURS

The *Catechism of the Catholic Church* defines faith as:

> ...a personal adherence of man to God. At the same
> time and inseparably, it is a free assent to the whole
> truth that God has revealed...[1]

In that definition, three elements present themselves: objective truths to be believed, the subjective act of belief on the part of the individual, and a self-surrender, in which a person completely allows God to take possession of his or her life. This is the make-up of all believers, and Thérèse was no exception. In our lives of faith, we may learn many lessons from hers.

The twenty-first century is anything but an age of faith. Social concern, personal economic success, the pursuit of the good life, moral pragmatism, etc., are all characteristic, but lives centered in God are few and far between. In many ways, these times do not differ from the nineteenth century as much as might be thought. Saint Thérèse grew up in a world greatly affected by the Enlightenment, a rejection of faith in the name of science and reason. The political world knew Karl Marx, the moral order was influenced by Sigmund Freud, and the study of philosophy

---

[1] *Catechism of the Catholic Church*, (Liguori, MO: Liguori Publications, 1994), 40.

was tainted with Friedrich Nietzsche. Militant atheism abounded and anti-clericalism was rampant. In the midst of it all, we have the life of a young girl in Lisieux, full of faith, trust in God, and absolute confidence. The study of that faith-filled life can teach everyone who chooses to listen how to be similarly faith-filled in today's apathetic, morally free culture.

Much of Thérèse's life of faith was centered in the wonderful parents God gave her, Louis and Zélie Martin, whose lives were great studies in sanctity. The home atmosphere at Les Buissonnets, as well as the liturgical life in the Cathedral of Saint-Pierre, each had its part to play in the child's development, as did her early years of formation at the Benedictine School in the town of Lisieux, a time in her life when she was often found totally absorbed in prayer. She thought constantly of heaven, without for a moment losing sight of the importance of preparing for it on this earth. In her *Last Conversations* she would mention it over sixty times, and more than seven hundred times in other writings. Looking back on her young sister's life of faith years later, Céline (Sister Genevieve of the Holy Face) reflected...

Everything, no matter how ordinary, helped to increase her faith, and purely secular things were for her an occasion of calling religious thoughts to mind. For instance, when our cousin Jeanne Guerin was getting married (which happened a week after she took the veil herself), she was impressed by all the little attentions she lavished on her fiancé, and immediately drew from it the lesson she must be just as assiduous in her attention to Jesus. Imitating Jeanne's wedding invitation, she even sent me an invitation to her own spiritual nuptials. Nature and artistic masterpieces raised her mind to God too. Particularly on her journey to Rome, she hardly knew how to express the beauty of the countryside, the splendor of the buildings, the fineness of the paintings and sculpture, or the melodiousness of the language.... The Servant of God's spirit of faith made her see God's will in all her trials, and thus rendered them clear to her. On the occasion of our father's illness, she wrote to me... that "Jesus has given us a loving look, a tear-veiled look, and this look has become for us an ocean of suffering, but also an ocean of grace and love." This spirit of faith made her see God's hand even in the most human situations. As she wrote to me: "God alone orders the events of this life of ours in exile. But we don't see Him; He hides Himself and we see only creatures.... Creatures are steps, or instruments, but it is the hand of Jesus that guides everything." And whatever Sister Thérèse taught me, she practiced it herself.[2]

Such a deep faith accounted for so pronounced a love of God, and faith is not really faith if it is not tested. Thérèse would be put to the test on many occasions, and she would also put her faith to work in constantly beseeching the "good God" for particular favors. As a young girl, her faith was tried and well tested by a period of intense scrupulosity — at an age when most children would hardly be affected by such concerns. So great was her love of God, however, that she was terribly concerned that the slightest action on her part might hurt Him. A traditional Catholic understanding of this problem has been defined as:

---

[2] Christopher O'Mahoney, *Saint Thérèse of Lisieux by Those Who Knew Her* (Dublin: Veritas, 1975), 123-124.

...[a] source of difficulty in determining what is right or fitting. An excessive severe judgment on one's own conduct based on an erroneous conscience.[3]

If the conscience of Saint Thérèse was in any way misdirected, it was surely not out of fear, but rather out of love. The problem seems to have originated during a school retreat when she was listening to a conference on mortal sin, preached by one Abbé Domin. The young girl resolved not to become discouraged, to recite the *Memorare* to Our Lady each day, and, where necessary, to humble her pride. Despite all these good intentions, the force of the preacher's rhetoric proved too overwhelming, and the more she dwelled on his message, the more fearful she became. Her mother was long gone. Pauline, her first mother, was in Carmel (and she could not confide her deepest fears to her sister in the parlor of a convent), hence she turned to Marie, her second mother, still at home. To her sister she continually poured out her deepest fears, her most absurd thoughts, all the particulars troubling her, concerns more than likely associated with purity, a very taboo subject in the Normandy of her day, and an area in which several of her siblings, by their own admission, experienced similar difficulties. Marie patiently listened to her young sister as she painstakingly went over every detail, and, apparently proved a fine source of encouragement. This scrupulosity was to last eighteen months, a "terrible disease," as she called it, and always credited the intercession of her four siblings in heaven with bringing it to an end. "You would have to endure this martyrdom to understand what it was like," Thérèse wrote,

---

[3] Albert J. Nevins, MM (ed.), *The Maryknoll Catholic Dictionary* (New York: Grosset & Dunlap, 1965), 516.

"it would be impossible for me to say what I suffered for eighteen months."[4] The fact that such difficulties passed may be one of the most convincing proofs of her abiding faith.

Another episode attesting to her confidence and trust in God involved the somewhat unlikely character, Henri Pranzini, whose exploits captured the headlines of the major French newspapers as well as many of those on the Continent. In March, 1887, two women and a young girl were brutally murdered on the streets of Paris. One woman was notorious in the French capital for her fast living, and the girl was thought to be her daughter, the other woman a maid. The trail led to Pranzini, who was apprehended in Marseilles and brought to trial, convicted and sentenced to death. The young Thérèse read every detail of the case in Parisian newspapers, and began to storm heaven for some sign of repentance on the part of Pranzini before he met his Creator. She began to sacrifice, to pray, and she even asked her sister Céline to have Masses offered for a special intention, though she did not divulge any particulars.

> I was convinced in the depths of my heart that our desires would be granted, but to give me courage to go on praying for sinners I told God I was sure He would pardon poor unfortunate Pranzini and that I would believe it even if he did not go to confession or show any sign of repentance. I had such confidence in Jesus' infinite mercy, but I was asking for a "sign" of repentance just for my own consolation.[5]

---

[4] Cited in Guy Gaucher, OCD, *The Story of a Life* (New York: HarperCollins), 1993, 55.

[5] Ibid., 67.

That sign was given her on August 31, 1887. It was the day of Pranzini's execution, and he had refused any ministrations of a priest. Then, a strange thing happened: as he was being led to the gallows to be hung, he turned and asked to be given a crucifix. When one was provided, he kissed it twice. When Thérèse read this account after Pranzini's death, she was overjoyed; her faith had told her God would somehow provide for Pranzini's salvation — this was proof to her He had done just that. She asked for a sign, and her intensity and sincerity in asking is a marvelous lesson to all believers that when we approach the good Lord in similar fashion, whatever the end result, He is never outdone in generosity.

If there was ever a trial of faith which weighed heavily on the mind and in the heart of Saint Thérèse, it was the declining health of the father for whom she had such deep affection, Louis Martin. No doubt it was heightened by the rumors circulating throughout Lisieux that the entrance of his daughters, but especially his youngest daughter, was the cause of such rapid deterioration. Yet the facts themselves caused the young nun's faith to be tested, and developed to great maturity. In late June, 1888, a little more than two months after Thérèse had entered Carmel, her father had left home without telling anyone. Two days later, a letter was postmarked from Le Havre, to Céline, asking that she send her father some money. All of this was very uncharacteristic of such a responsible man, and quite naturally alarmed Céline, who, in company with her uncle Isidore Guerin and another friend, went to Le Havre in search of Monsieur Martin. They began searching at the Post Office, where they thought he might be looking for them. He was found the day after their arrival, and it was determined he was suffering from arteriosclerosis, a disease which restricts the flow of blood to the brain and legs. It was already causing him to have periods of forgetfulness and hallucinations.

Much of his life went on in normal fashion until October 31st, at Honfleur, when he suffered a serious relapse. The following January 10th, Thérèse received the habit of the Carmelite Order, though her father was unable to attend the ceremony. Within two weeks he began to suffer bouts of over-stimulation and drowsiness; nonetheless, at the end of the month he was able to go to Alençon on business. That would be his last visit to the town he once called home, and shortly after his return to Lisieux he was confined to bed. One author who studied the course of his illness noted that at this stage…

> The cerebral paralysis grew worse. His brain was impaired. He had lapses of memory. His imagination played tricks on him. He thought he was seeing frightful things, slaughter and battles. He could hear the sound of cannons and drums. Having heard about a robbery in the town, [he] then wanted to carry his revolver with him at all times to defend his home and family.[6]

By now, February, 1889, the decision was made to place this very holy man into the care of the sisters at Bon Sauveur Hospital in Caen, where they looked after the mentally ill. The months went by, and both Leonie and Céline, along with uncle Isidore, made frequent trips to see him. In May, his brother-in-law was able to bring him to LaMusse, a country home that the Guerin family had purchased some time earlier. After a vacation period he seemed to enjoy, his life resumed at Bon Sauveur, his

---

[6] Paulinus Redmond, *Louis and Zélie Martin: The Seed and the Root of the Little Flower* (London: Quiller Press, 1995), 253.

condition varying from week to week. A paralysis of his lower limbs continuously progressed, so that by Easter, 1890, he could hardly stand upright. Thérèse was professed in September, but, once again, Monsieur Martin was in no condition to be present. Céline took the crown she was to wear at the ceremony for him to bless and place on his forehead; he also kissed the crucifix she was to wear after her profession, and he was shown the paper with the written vows which she held during the profession ceremony. Shortly before her own death, Thérèse revealed to Pauline...

> I was obliged to ask for Papa's cure on the day of my profession; however, it was impossible for me to say anything else but this: "My God, I beg you, let it be your will that Papa be cured."[7]

Louis Martin did not will that himself; when he heard from Céline that the entire family was making a novena to Saint Joseph that he be cured, he asked that they pray only that the will of God be done.

In May, 1892, Isidore Guerin was able to bring Monsieur Martin back to Lisieux, not to Les Buissonnets, but to a smaller residence the family had taken. Two days later, he was taken to the Carmel to see his three daughters.

> He seemed to be aware of everything that was taking place. He could hardly speak, but just before leaving, he raised his eyes, pointed upwards and simply said "In heaven."[8]

The point he was trying to make was that they would all meet again, some day, in heaven. It would not be long in coming

---

[7]   Ibid., 258-259.

[8]   Ibid., 262.

for this gentleman who had once been one of the leading citizens of Lisieux. His mind was affected by frequent seizures, which made him appear childish at times. In February, 1893, he was cognizant enough to realize that Pauline had been elected Prioress of the Carmel, and to delight in the fact that his daughter was so honored. His death came on July 29, 1894, while on a summer trip to La Musse. Four days later, he was buried from the Cathedral of Saint-Pierre in Lisieux.

Thérèse received news of her father's death in silence. There is no record of any immediate reaction or statement she made. It was not until later that summer she began to share with her sisters some of her feelings. She felt her father's presence very strongly; after a death lasting nearly five years, she felt that now in heaven, the family patriarch was once again trying to do everything he could for his daughters. For the six years she'd been in Carmel, she was acutely aware of his absence; now having taken his place in the Communion of Saints, she knew her father was present to her in a way he had never been before.

A discussion with her sister, Sister Marie of the Sacred Heart, is particularly revealing. She harkened back to a childhood memory from Les Buissonnets; at the time it had scared her — only in the aftermath of her father's passing did it begin to make sense. The story involved a vision she experienced at the age of six or seven:

> From her window Thérèse said she had seen a man dressed exactly like Papa, bent over and covering his head with a sort of apron, cross the bottom of the garden and disappear behind a hedge. Had Victoire [the maid] been playing a practical joke? The maid denied it; she had not left her kitchen. The shrubs were thor-

oughly searched. Nothing. The mystery remained. Her sisters tried to reassure the child.... It took fourteen years for the Martins, who were then Carmelites, to understand the meaning of that mysterious happening.[9]

Thérèse put it succinctly:

As Jesus' adorable face was veiled during His passion, in the same way was the face of His faithful servant veiled during the days of his sufferings, so that he would be able to shine in the heavenly home with his Lord, the eternal Word![10]

Perhaps the one episode from her brief life which most clearly underscores her faith occurred near the end of her life, and was directly related to the first hemorrhage of blood she experienced on Good Friday, 1896:

...At that time, I was enjoying such a living faith, that the thought of heaven made up all my happiness, and I was unable to believe there were really impious people who had no faith.... He permitted my soul to be invaded by the thickest darkness, and that the thought of heaven, up to then so sweet to me, be no longer anything but the cause of struggle and torment.... The trial was to last not a few days or a few weeks, it was not to be extinguished until the hour set by God himself, and this hour has not yet come.[11]

---

[9] Gaucher, op. cit., 38.
[10] Cited in ibid., 134.
[11] Cited in Christopher O'Donnell, O.Carm., *Love in the Heart of the Church* (Dublin: Veritas, 1997), 168-169.

Thérèse refers to the intense spiritual trial that will accompany her final illness. The two would go hand in hand until September 30, 1897, when she breathed her last, telling God how much she loved Him. It is little short of amazing that during this period of her life she completed Manuscripts B and C of her autobiography; she wrote a total of eighteen letters to her two priest brothers — eleven to Maurice Bellière, and seven to Adolph Roulland. There is a great lesson to be learned for all willing to listen: keep going in the midst of life's difficulties with confidence in God's love and ever abiding grace.

How did Thérèse herself deal with this ultimate test of her faith? First of all, by identifying herself with sinners and unbelievers, and offering her sufferings for them.

> …Your child, O Lord, has understood your divine light, and she begs pardon for her brothers. She is resigned to eat the bread of sorrow as long as you desire it; she does not want to rise up from this table filled with bitterness at which poor sinners are eating until the day set by you.[12]

There is decided resignation in her words. She knows there are so many people so much worse than herself, ranging from those with doubts of faith to those who have given up its active practice. In this, Thérèse appears to be telling all who study her, no matter what struggles might arise, there are always people in more dire straits. There is great consolation in the fact that the entire community of believers is undergoing some test, or trial or difficulty. Such knowledge deepens our awareness of the Lord's

---

[12] Ibid.

THE SAINT FOR THE THIRD MILLENNIUM: THÉRÈSE OF LISIEUX

own goodness to ourselves, and with such appreciation, faith cannot help but be strengthened.

The fact remained that the trial of Thérèse did not let up, and would not let up. Mother Agnes was very clear on this in her testimony at Thérèse's beatification process:

> …Her soul remained until the end plunged in a veritable night, because of her temptation against the existence of heaven.[13]

Thérèse was at pains to note that only those who have walked through the dark tunnel can really appreciate how dark the darkness can be. Even brief moments of respite did little to alleviate the temptation to doubt.

> It is true that at times a very small ray of sun comes to illuminate my darkness, and then the trial ceases for an instant, but afterwards, the memory of that ray, instead of causing me joy, makes my darkness even more dense.[14]

Throughout her writings she uses terms such as a wall, a darkness, a tunnel, a thick fog, and the like. Yet, she did not share her trial with many people; her fellow Carmelites surely did not know it; in fact, most would have guessed just the opposite. She had so perfected what one author has called the spirituality of the smile, that the members of her community, rather than realizing the torments she was enduring, were actually uplifted from the difficulties of their own lives by her very presence.

---

[13] Ibid., 170.
[14] Ibid., 172.

One particular day, Thérèse had very serious temptations against the existence of heaven — far worse than usual. Years later, Mother Agnes recalled that she kept repeating over and over the lines of a poem she had written:

> Since the Son of God wished His Mother
> To undergo darkness and heartfelt anguish
> Mary, is it therefore a good thing to suffer on earth?
> Yes, to suffer out of love is purest happiness
> Jesus can take back everything He has given me,
> But tell Him never to get angry with me
> He can hide if He likes, and I will wait for Him
> Till that undying day when my faith will cease to be[15]

She responded to her trial of faith by offering them for sinners, and also for priests, one of the most important components of her spiritual life. Also, on the recommendation of a retreat master to whom she confided her trial of faith, she wrote out the Apostles Creed, carried it around with her, and recited it several times throughout the day, especially at those moments she needed it the most. She delved into the merciful love of God as she prepared the heart of her autobiography, confiding to her sister Marie that she was not "swimming in consolations," rather her greatest consolation was to "have none on earth." Finally, she wanted to enter as deeply as possible into the transforming love of Jesus by learning to love her own littleness, because in that littleness was to be found greatness:

---

[15] O'Mahoney, op. cit., 41.

> Let us love to feel nothing… then Jesus will come
> to look for us… and however far we may be He will
> transform us with flames of love. Oh, how I would like
> to be able to make you understand what I feel.[16]

Thérèse's' reference to flames of love indicates the strong influence the writings of the sixteenth century Spanish Carmelite St. John of the Cross had on her. She took him as a spiritual guide and begged God to work the same transformation in her that was described in his classic work, *The Living Flame of Love*, to be able, as she put it, to love until death. In the months prior to her death, confined to the infirmary in Carmel, she continued to read and take notes on John's writings. She did not adopt his imagery, preferring instead to concentrate on the central message of the gospel, the passion of Christ. Nonetheless, from what she had learned she could offer her three sisters some important recommendations on remaining firmly rooted in faith.

> Don't be astonished if I don't appear to you after my
> death, and if you see nothing extraordinary as a sign
> of my happiness. You will remember that it's 'my little
> way' not to desire to see anything.[17]

Saint John of the Cross, her own prayerful meditation on scripture, her "little way" all combined to teach her that faith does not require extraordinary signs. She was not looking for any, nor does she encourage her followers to. Her faith told her very

---

[16] Thérèse to Sister Marie of the Sacred Heart, 17 September, 1896, cited in O'Donnell, op. cit., 175.

[17] Cited in Guy Gaucher, *The Passion of Thérèse of Lisieux* (New York: Crossroad Publishing Company, 1998), 223.

clearly what awaited her, and even in the midst of the temptations she endured, she expected nothing more than the death her Lord had suffered.

> Our Lord died on the Cross in agony, and yet this is the most beautiful death of love. This is the only one that was seen. No one saw the Blessed Virgin die. To die of love is not to die in transports. I tell you frankly, it seems to me that this is what I am experiencing.[18]

Few people in the course of the Church's life have clung to their faith so tenaciously amid such a variety of circumstances. It is easy to point to the sanctity of Thérèse, and easily distance oneself from any sort of comparison with one's own life. At such moments, the thought must also occur that every event of the young saint's life speaks to our own. She had every right to pray the prayer, "Lord, I believe; help my unbelief." If, in her humanness, she learned to strengthen her faith through the happenings of her life, should anyone who follows the Lord really expect to do less?

---

[18] Ibid., 224.

CHAPTER SIX

PRAYING WITH SAINT THÉRÈSE

In Scranton, Pennsylvania, the Episcopal Residence of the Bishop of the Diocese is located next to Saint Peter's Cathedral, in the center of the city. On the second floor of this imposing structure is a very beautiful chapel called the Oratory of the Little Flower. The three windows behind the Altar of Sacrifice are of special note. The first depicts Saint Thérèse kneeling before Our Blessed Mother, who is holding the Divine Child — it is the same depiction as the banner that was unfurled at Saint Peter's in Rome on the day of her canonization. In the center, Saint Thérèse the sacristan, copied from a famous photograph of the young Sister with the sacred vessels. The final window is the equally well known depiction of the young girl kneeling at the feet of Pope Leo XIII, asking for permission to enter Carmel at the age of fifteen. To the right of these windows is a statue of the Saint holding a large number of roses, evoking memories of her promise to intercede until the world is no more. When one comes into the presence of Our Lord in the Blessed Sacrament in this chapel, one is immediately filled with thoughts of the importance of prayer — in this case, praying to Thérèse for her intercession, and praying with Thérèse to the God she loved so much.

The importance of prayer for everyone was brought out very well some years ago in the play, *Shadowlands*, the life of the

Christian apologist, C.S. Lewis. In one scene, Lewis is telling a friend how often he prayed, adding that if he ever stopped praying, he believed he would stop living. The friend responded with the observation that Lewis' prayers must be working, since his wife appeared to be improving. Lewis agreed, but said that was not the reason he prayed; he prayed because of a need flowing out of him, and when he prayed, he felt it changed him. Lewis must have been surprised when his friend told him that was the first sensible point he had ever heard on prayer.

The dialogue itself presents a teachable moment, though one cannot escape the thought that had Lewis' friend been in the habit of reading Saint Thérèse, he would hear her make many sensible points on prayer. She never spoke about it from some lofty pedestal; she is one of us, and she experienced the same difficulties so many faithful souls know all too well. Carmelite Father Christopher O'Donnell, writing on the subject of Saint Thérèse and prayer, describes such situations:

> Aridity (dryness) is… a certain powerlessness during prayer to elicit thoughts or affections about spiritual things. This powerlessness can be the fault of the person praying, perhaps some infidelity, serious resistance to grace, general tepidity or lukewarmness in serving God. It may also come from circumstances, such as external worries, physical or psychological weakness, or it may be a trial sent by God that purifies and strengthens the person. Dryness in practice is the absence of what makes prayer easy, so that, despite efforts, there is no longer any relish in prayer. One cannot surface appropriate thoughts; one experiences being empty or void during prayer. If one knows the reason for this

problem and can do something about its causes, then it may be relieved. In many cases it just comes, and the only remedy is to remain faithful to the times of prayer. Such dryness is absolutely necessary for spiritual growth. When it is nice to pray, we may be only pleasing ourselves and enjoying the satisfaction we obtain. It is when prayer becomes dry and even almost impossible that our love is purified and we pray not for our own satisfaction but for God.[1]

Such difficulties were not at all foreign to Thérèse. There were only two recorded times in her life when an overwhelming sense of the love of the Lord seemed to envelop her; once, as a child, in the presence of the "Virgin of the Smile," and years later, in Carmel, when she was making the stations of the Cross, and deeply meditating on the Lord's passion. Aside from that, her lot is exactly the same as so many others who must keep trying.

> Sometimes when my mind is in such a great aridity that it is impossible to draw forth one single thought to unite me with God, I very slowly recite an Our Father and then the angelic salutation; then these prayers give me great delight; they nourish my soul much more than if I had recited them precipitately a hundred times.[2]

This marvelous young saint knows exactly what many people who want to pray more fervently go through. We can identify

---

[1] Christopher O'Donnell, O.Carm., *Prayer: Insights from St. Thérèse of Lisieux* (Dublin: Veritas, 2001), 93-94.

[2] John Clarke, OCD (trans.), *Story of a Soul: The Autobiography of Saint Thérèse of Lisieux* (Washington, DC: ICS Publications, 1996), 243.

with her, and she with us. For all of her wonderful insights into prayer, Thérèse faced many of the same struggles we do. If she is close to us in our struggles of faith, she is also close to us in our struggles in prayer. She never stopped trying; she never slackened in her attempts to draw closer to the God she loved, and the God who loved her.

> Prayer is not just something that one does by inclination when one feels in the mood for prayer; prayer is also a matter of disciplines and habits faithfully practiced and persisted in, even when one does not feel "in the mood." We are not just intellectuals, and it is not with our minds alone that we believe or pray. In the school of prayer which was her home, Thérèse learned that prayer is discipline, as well as spontaneity, that prayer is rule as well as love, it is an acquired and practiced habit as well as mood and sentiment and joy. Indeed, spontaneity in prayer is the fruit of discipline; it results from regular and rule regulated habitual practice. The love and joy of praying are granted only to those who pray even when there is no inclination to pray and no felt joy in praying.[3]

One of the most convincing proofs that Thérèse is a great teacher of prayer is the fact that her definition of it is cited in the *Catechism of the Catholic Church*. A more elaborate understanding will be found in her own autobiography:

---

[3] Cardinal Cathal B. Daly, *Thérèse: A Saint for all Seasons* (Kildare Town: Thérèsian International Congress, 1997, Unpublished Paper).

One could call it a Queen who has at each instant free access to the King and who is able to obtain whatever she asks. To be heard it is not necessary to read from a book some beautiful formula composed for the occasion. If this were the case, alas, I would have to be pitied! Outside the Divine Office which I am very unworthy to recite, I do not have the courage to force myself to search out beautiful prayers in books. There are so many of them it really gives me a headache! and each prayer is more beautiful than the others. I cannot recite them all, and not knowing which to choose, I do like children who do not know how to read, I say very simply to God what I wish to say, without composing beautiful sentences, and He always understands me. For me, prayer is an aspiration of the heart, it is a simple glance directed to heaven, it is a cry of gratitude and love in the midst of trial as well as joy; finally, it is something great, supernatural, which expands my soul and unites me to Jesus.[4]

Her heart began aspiring when she was very young. She once recalled a fishing expedition with her father, sitting on the green grass of a river bank. At that age she had no idea what meditation was, but she began to feel that the life she was living was not the life for which she was made — the earth, it seemed, was a mere place of exile where we spent only a limited amount of time. Heaven was her true homeland, and one detects sadness in her being separated from the place she really should be. The fact that this thought was persistent and so deeply felt is a remarkable

---

4   Clarke, op. cit., 242.

insight into God's grace in her young life, and clearly shows what she meant by aspiration. Her reaction to the beauties of the world around her is also indication of that same aspiration.

> I was six or seven years old when Papa brought us to Trouville. Never will I forget the impression the sea made upon me; I couldn't take my eyes off it since its majesty, the roaring of its waves, everything spoke to my soul of God's grandeur and power.[5]

There is a beautiful window in the Church of Our Lady of Victories in Paris depicting Thérèse and her father deep in prayer. They went to this famous Paris church in 1887 as the first stop on a diocesan pilgrimage that brought them to many parts of Italy, and finally to Rome, where a fourteen-year-old girl had a very famous encounter with Pope Leo XIII. As you meditate on the expressions of the girl and her father in that window, you find yourself thinking, that, too, is aspiration.

Thérèse always described herself as a simple soul, and shied away from much formality in her prayer life. Her way to God is very simple and direct, and you do not find an emphasis on degrees or stages as is often the case in the other Carmelite masters, John of the Cross and Teresa of Avila. Though her approach was less formal, she loved the formal setting of adoration of the Blessed Sacrament. Her father had been a member of the Guild of the Blessed Sacrament in Lisieux, and had introduced her to praying before Our Lord exposed on the altar from the time she was very young. As a Carmelite, she composed much of her extant writings and many of her letters and poems in the presence of the Blessed Sacrament in the convent chapel.

---

[5] Ibid., 48.

A very important question to consider is how her "aspiration of the heart" worked — what were the particulars that stimulated her own assent to God? *The Imitation of Christ* in her younger life, and, to a very great extent, Scripture in her later years. We were not living in a period of the Church's history when the study of, or meditation on, Holy Writ was emphasized, or for that matter, encouraged. In this, Thérèse anticipated the Second Vatican Council by seventy years.

Over half a century ago, the late Monsignor Thomas Bird, Professor of Scripture at Oscott College in England, wrote an essay on Saint Thérèse's use of the Bible. In researching his topic, he wrote to the Lisieux Carmel to discover how Thérèse had such a grasp of, and love for God's word. The response he received is revealing, not only of the Saint herself, but also the Carmelite community:

> Our Mother has very kindly helped me to reply to your question about Saint Thérèse and her knowledge of the Bible. Our Mother has told me to tell you that every sister in Carmel has one hour each day — sometimes more — in which she may read, study or pray; that each sister has a New Testament; and with permission and discretion, the sisters may have a Bible in their cells, or borrow one from the library; that evidently Saint Thérèse had this permission and must have studied in the free time. But there is no obligation to read or study in Carmel — we are left quite free on these points.[6]

---

[6] Thomas Bird, DD, PhD, "Saint Thérèse and the Scriptures" in Michael Day (ed.), *Christian Simplicity in St. Thérèse* (London: Burns Oates, 1953), 124.

Monsignor Bird was still puzzled: how could Thérèse have developed to the point she did? Bird was teaching seminarians; he found in the young Carmelite nun an understanding vastly superior to men preparing for the priesthood and exposed to far more formal study of the Old and New Testaments than any religious sister of the late nineteenth century would have been.

> [S]he knew the church's teaching on biblical matters with astonishing accuracy. She knew that the sacred Books were divinely inspired and that they were free from error; she studied the literal and historical sense first of all, but she did not stop there; she went on to "discover" new lights and mysterious hidden meanings. Thereby she followed the method of the best exponents of the sacred text.... [S]he knew the Scriptures so easily that the right quotations simply flowed from her pen with a facility that is quite difficult to understand if we seek for merely natural explanations.[7]

Years earlier, a contemporary account bore striking similarity to Monsignor Bird's. In 1894, Thérèse had been made Mistress of Novices, and of all the younger sisters she directed, she was closest to, and most strongly influenced Sister Marie of the Trinity. This young novice, born Marie Louise Josephine Castel at Saint Pierre sur Dives in the Diocese of Bayeux in 1874, was the thirteenth of nineteen children. Upon her entrance, her thinking was a bit superficial, but, once introduced to the Little Way, she arrived at a very high degree of spiritual perfection. Testifying at the beatification process, she brought to the fore some very revealing insights about Thérèse:

---

[7] Ibid., 126-128.

...I am very sorry that I did not note down systematically all the lights which she received in prayer and passed on to me for the good of my soul. She had an extraordinary ability for interpreting the Scriptures. She was so good at discovering the beauty of all these holy books that it was as if they no longer held any secrets for her. One day during prayer she was particularly struck by the passage in the Song of Songs where the spouse says to the beloved 'We shall make you chains of gold inlaid with silver.' 'What a strange thing for the spouse to say,' she said, 'you would expect a silver chain inlaid with gold, or a gold chain inlaid with precious stones, because usually a piece of jewelry is inlaid with something more precious than itself. But Jesus has given me the key to the mystery: He has shown me that the gold chains are love, charity, but that He does not like them unless they are inlaid with the silver of childlike simplicity'.[8]

In her autobiography, *The Story of a Soul*, there are more than one hundred thirty scriptural references, and numerous other allusions. Thirteen books of the Old Testament are cited. From the New Testament, the gospels in particular, and many of the Pauline letters, especially Saint Paul's Letter to the Romans, and his First Letter to the Corinthians. She continually emphasized powerlessness to climb to God, and her complete dependency on His mercy and love. These thoughts came to her from the Books of Proverbs and Wisdom, as well as from the Prophet Isaiah. In

---

[8] Christopher O'Mahoney (ed.), *St. Thérèse of Lisieux by Those Who Knew Her* (Dublin: Veritas, 1975), 236.

First Corinthians, she found her own vocation, to be love in the heart of the Church.

When Thérèse was in Rome for Pope Leo XIII's jubilee, she went to visit the Church of Saint Cecilia in Trastevere and prayed at the tomb of this early Roman martyr. She quoted a verse of a hymn of Saint Cecilia that made reference to the gospel resting on the saint's heart. Thérèse may well have emulated that, because she would write out verses of Scripture and pin them to her habit, close to her heart as it were, committing them to memory, and coming closer to God by such continuous repetition. Also, she copied and compared texts, and was able to quote effortlessly from them.

In what have become known as her *Last Conversations*, she looked back on all God had done for her. One of His greatest gifts was allowing His word to truly penetrate her heart:

> [W]ith the exception of the Gospels, I no longer find anything in books. The Gospels are enough. I listen with delight to these words of Jesus which tell me all I must do: 'Learn of me for I am meek and humble of heart'; then I'm at peace, according to His sweet promise: 'and you will find rest for your souls.'[9]

Thérèse took the example of Our Lord in Scripture, to go off and commune with His heavenly Father in private. That could have meant whatever form privacy would have afforded her, but most often, it was the privacy of her own mind and heart in the presence of Our Lord in the Blessed Sacrament. She always felt her time of prayer was really the Lord's time — it was her total

---

[9] John Clarke, OCD (trans.), *St. Thérèse of Lisieux: Her Last Conversations* (Washington, DC: ICS Publications, 1977), 44.

surrender to Him, and it was something that pleased Him immensely, regardless of her disposition at any given moment. She compared her prayer to the sacrifice of the Lord Jesus on Calvary — a self-giving love. As such, it was a joyful gift of herself, her very special gift to Him.

She always spoke of distractions, but as her life was coming to a close, far more than simple distractions plagued her. Her physical condition coupled with her inner torments about heaven made everything darkness and a void. By then, she could only offer a prayer of self surrender, and it has been suggested by those who have studied her inner life, that this prayer may have been God's ultimate gift. Although Thérèse never wrote a great deal about prayer, or how to pray, her legacy to all who would like to pray more fervently is found in the example of her all-abiding love of God's word, and her persistence in concentrating on that word. When Pope John Paul II traveled to Lisieux as a pilgrim in 1980, his words were well chosen:

> Of Saint Thérèse of Lisieux, it can be said with conviction that the Spirit of God let her reveal directly, to the men and women of our time, the fundamental mystery, the reality of the Gospel: the fact that we have really received a "spirit of adoption which makes us cry out: Abba, Father!" And, indeed, what truth of the Gospel is more fundamental and more universal than this: God is our Father and we are His children?[10]

While Scripture was surely one of her great nourishments, the question could be asked, in what way did it nourish her?

---

[10] Cited in Eugene McCaffrey, OCD, *Heart of Love* (Dublin: Veritas, 1998), 28.

For what, specifically, did she pray? Some of the answers to that question are as obvious as the intentions for which we all pray; perseverance, growth in the love of God, our loved ones, those with whom we live and work, the world in which we live, etc. That would have been the case for Thérèse as well, but she was very specific about why she had to come to Carmel: to save souls, and to pray for priests, and even more specifically, to pray for missionary priests, and, by extension, to pray for the mission of the Church. There is no question that her life of prayer was significantly enhanced by the correspondence she had with her two missionary priest brothers, Maurice Bellière and Adolph Roulland. She saw her task as drawing both of them closer to the merciful love of God.

> …[S]he moved very quickly to be their spiritual friend, indeed their guide. Her letters are strong, at times stern, but always loving calls to holiness. She genuinely hoped that they would be martyrs! She invited them to nothing less than she herself had discovered — total abandonment to God and confidence in His mercy and love.[11]

Less than three years after her canonization, she was proclaimed Co-Patroness of the Missions of the Church with Saint Francis Xavier. The reason for this was completely spiritual — she felt that the best way for Carmelites to be useful to the Church was by prayer and sacrifice. She was not simply dedicating her life to prayer, but to this specific prayer, and the origins of it were to be found in her young childhood. One Sunday at Mass, as she

[11] O'Donnell, op. cit., 108.

was closing her missal, a holy card slipped on to the floor. It was a picture of the Crucifixion, and she immediately thought how regrettable it was that so many gave such little thought to the Lord's sacrifice, personal as it is for every soul. She then and there resolved she would spend her life making amends for this lack.

> My heart was pierced with sorrow to see the precious blood falling with no one bothering to catch it, and I made up my mind… to stay in spirit at the foot of the cross, to gather up the dew of heavenly life and give it to others. From that moment the cry of the dying Saviour 'I thirst,' echoed in my heart and I longed to satisfy His thirst for souls.[12]

As a young girl en route to Rome, someone gave her a copy of a publication called *Missionary Annals*, but she was quick to pass it on to Céline. The life of missionary activity held no interest for her, even then. She desired the cloistered life, where she could accomplish far more. In her early convent years, there was serious discussion of her going to help establish a Carmel in Hanoi, North Vietnam, where she would have joined other sisters from the Carmel in Saigon (begun from Lisieux in 1861). Talk of it diminished for awhile, but surfaced again in 1896, after her deteriorating health seemed to be showing signs of significant improvement. Thérèse began a novena to the martyr Theophane Venard, for whom she had a strong devotion. She was asking for a sign of God's will, and her answer was quick in coming. Half way through the novena, she experienced a recurrence of the coughing that had plagued her — this time far more seriously. She

---

[12] Cited in McCaffrey, op. cit., 53-54.

would not go to Southeast Asia, but instead would concentrate her efforts on her two missionary brothers, by praying for them with greater intensity, and corresponding with them on matters of holiness. She had not felt such happiness in years; the thought of the good she might accomplish in their lives, with God's grace, filled her with joy. She compared the feeling to a musical chord within her that had not been struck for a very long time. The letters she wrote to Fathers Bellière and Roulland contain her deepest missionary insights, and serve as spiritual food for anyone concerned with the spread of the gospel.

> Thérèse is an Apostle, an Evangelist — in a word, a Missionary. She was consumed with the desire to convert others. "To love Jesus and to make others love Him" was the motto of her life and its whole purpose. "Aimez Jesus et Le faire aimer." How often she said it. She could not abide the thought that souls be lost, and she wanted to travel the whole world to proclaim the Gospel to everyone, the Gospel, the Good News of God's merciful love. It grieved her that so many people did not know of God's love for them.... She was a missionary par excellence who never thought of herself but only of others.... One mission, she said, would never be enough for her. She wanted to labor in every mission until every soul was saved. She spoke of that desire as a folly, but it was no folly at all. The same desire obsessed the heart of Jesus, who shed his blood on the Cross for the salvation of everyone.[13]

---

[13] Bishop Patrick V. Ahern, St. Thérèse: Patroness of the Missions (New York: The Society for the Propagation of the Faith, undated), 3-4.

Far better than traveling the world, she knew well, was what she could accomplish in the Carmel of Lisieux.

> During her last illness the infirmarian suggested that she take a short walk in the garden each day. One of the sisters noticed how much effort this cost her and advised her to rest. 'It is true,' Thérèse replied, 'it is an effort, but do you know what gives me strength? I offer each step for some missionary, thinking that somewhere far away, one of them is worn out from his labors and, to lessen his fatigue, I offer mine to God.'[14]

That is why she is Co-Patroness of the Missions, because of the efficacy of those prayers! And to each of us, Thérèse has much to say on prayer: it is an aspiration of all our hearts, time spent with God, not our time, but His. Time in which we pour out our hearts to Him, not with a long harangue of formal prayers, but as the Spirit of Christ prompts us: making use of God's word, spending time in His presence, and doing this over and over again, never tiring, never letting go. How easily Thérèse would have identified with the realism of the English Benedictine Dom John Chapman, who continually reminded his readers, the less we pray, the worse it goes.

---

[14] McCaffrey, op. cit., 55.

CHAPTER SEVEN

THÉRÈSE AND SUFFERING

If we take seriously the Lord's admonition to take up our cross and follow Him, few of us, if any at all, will be exempt from suffering in this life. Thérèse was no exception, and she would experience suffering on three levels — physical, emotional, and psychological. Her life is proof positive that all bear the cross, but particulars differ from one human being to another. Many think their cross is hard — purely because it is theirs. Those given to others seem insignificant by comparison, but they are not. One spiritual writer notes that "every cross in the world is tailor-made, custom-built, patterned to fit one and no one else."[1]

For centuries upon centuries before the coming of Our Lord, writers, poets, philosophers, and holy men and women had wrestled with the question of suffering and evil, its presence in the world and why God allowed it. Our Old Testament forebears saw meaning in it; the Book of Genesis viewed it as a punishment for sin, and the Psalms and Wisdom Literature seem to enforce this idea when they emphasize the fact that the good prosper while the evil suffer. On the other hand, the Book of Job's principal character is a good man who suffers, but places great trust in God in the midst of such travail. In the New Testament Letter to the

---

[1] Fulton J. Sheen, *Seven Words of Jesus and Mary* (Liguori, MO: Liguori/Triumph, 2001), 27.

Hebrews, suffering was seen to yield a fruit of healing, while Our Lord Himself, through His victimal offering of love, brought to fruition the songs of the Suffering Servant in the Book of the Prophet Isaiah. Hence, the most profound human response to suffering in the New Testament is the uniting of one's individual cross to that of Jesus Christ the Redeemer, described by Blaise Pascal as being on His cross until the end of the world. The greatest tragedy in an earthly life, then, is not what one suffers, but what one misses. Wasted pain seems one of the most common facts of so many lives. C.S. Lewis, in one of his works, said that God whispers to us in our pleasures, speaks to us in our conscience, and shouts to us in our pain. Long before he wrote that, a young woman in France was uniting her trials with those of her beloved in a way that would make her a saint — in a very short time.

> Sanctity does not consist in saying beautiful things;
> it does not even consist in thinking them, in feeling
> them. It consists in suffering, and suffering everything.
> (Sanctity! we must conquer it at the point of the sword;
> we must suffer… we must agonize). A day will come
> when the shadows will disappear.[2]

The mystery of suffering, like so many areas of the spiritual life, is one Thérèse knew intimately, and from her experience we may all learn. The word "trial" is found one hundred seventy-three times in her writings, the word "suffer" or "suffering," two hundred twenty-eight times. Almost half of these references are found in her correspondence, and very frequently she will speak of the "joy of suffering." In one particular missive written shortly

---

[2] Thérèse to Céline, 26 April, 1889. Cited in Christopher O'Donnell, O.Carm., *Love in the Heart of the Church* (Dublin: Veritas, 1997), 78.

before her death, she left no doubt that it was her desire to suffer, and, in light of the physical and spiritual torments she was enduring, such desire was not denied her. In 1895, as she began her autobiography, she focused on this very clearly:

> ...I find myself at a period of my life when I can cast a glance upon the past; my soul has matured in the crucible of exterior and interior trials, and now, like a flower strengthened by the storm, I can raise my head.[3]

Suffering may come to an individual in many forms; chiefly, it seems to appear in the psychological, spiritual, and physical areas of our lives, and Thérèse forcefully experienced it in all three.

Psychologically, it can be traced to her earliest childhood. At two and a half, she was sent to be nursed by a midwife, Rose Taille, who had also nursed two of the other Martin children. When she was four and a half, Thérèse's mother died in Alençon, and when Thérèse was nine, her sister Pauline, who had become her adopted mother, left for Carmel. Years later, she wrote of the impact this had on her:

> ...In one instance I understood what life was; until then I had never seen it so; but it appeared to me in all its reality, and I saw it was nothing but a continual suffering and separation. I shed bitter tears, because I did not yet understand the joy of sacrifice.[4]

---

[3] John Clarke, OCD (trans.), *Story of a Soul: The Autobiography of St. Thérèse of Lisieux* (Washington, DC: ICS Publications, 1996), 15.

[4] Ibid., 58.

Her separation from Pauline may have partially accounted for an illness which began in March, 1883, and concluded in May with the "smile" of the Blessed Virgin Mary emanating from a statue that had been placed near her sickbed in Les Buissonnets, and which, to this day, can be seen atop the saint's reliquary in a side oratory of the chapel of the Lisieux Carmel. Her symptoms began Easter Sunday evening; Thérèse and her sister Céline were staying with their uncle, Isidore Guerin, while their father, along with Marie and Leonie went to Paris for Holy Week. After she went to bed, she began to experience trembling, chills, agitation, etc. The next day, after a local physician recommended hydrotherapy, her father and sisters were hastily summoned from Paris and she was soon removed to her own home. During the next week, she was extremely sensitive, could rarely be left alone, experienced insomnia, rashes, fevers, and some failure of her motor nerves, that caused her, at times, to need help moving. Some years after these events, as testimony was being gathered for her beatification, Céline provided more detail on the particulars of her sister's illness:

> ...I felt I could recognize the devil's hand in this extraordinary illness; it was my own opinion and the opinion I heard expressed around me. In the course of it, I witnessed some terrifying scenes: she banged her head repeatedly off the wooden part of the bed (it was a big high bed) as if she was trying to kill herself; she used to stand up in bed, bend right down and execute a kind of somersault which, several times, caused her to go flying over the end of the bed and land heavily on the floor; the room had a stone floor, but she never harmed herself. One day I heard my uncle, M. Guerin,

a man of science and of faith, say that she would not be cured by human means. He had been house pharmacist to more than one hospital in Paris, and had seen some extraordinary cases in his day, but he said he had never seen one like this. He also reported that the Doctor had told him that Thérèse's case baffled medical science; that if these symptoms occurred in a girl of fourteen or fifteen they might perhaps be understood, but that they were totally inexplicable in a girl of ten. However, devotional objects did not frighten her, which is not the case in illnesses where the devil has a hand.... This illness lasted exactly five months; she was suddenly and completely cured on 10 May. When I saw the sudden change in her attitude and the expression on her face during the ecstasy, I had no doubt whatever she had seen the Blessed Virgin. I was so convinced of it, in fact, that I don't ever remember asking her to tell me about something which was so evident. But Marie did insist on her describing what she had seen.[5]

Thérèse came to yet a new dimension of suffering with her father's final illness and death. Louis Martin's struggle has been seen as part of this extraordinary young woman's life of faith, precisely because it entailed so much personal suffering for her. She was only fourteen when her father suffered his first paralysis, and following her entry to Carmel on April 9, 1888, a series of events seemed to intensify his emotional state; six weeks after Thérèse's departure, Marie took the veil on May 23rd; on June

---

[5] Christopher O'Mahoney (ed.), *St. Thérèse By Those Who Knew Her* (Dublin: Veritas, 1975), 152-153.

15th, Céline informed her father she wanted to enter Carmel, and at this same time, Leonie expressed a desire to give her vocation to the Visitandines at Le Mans. Happy as all these occurrences made Monsieur Martin, they undoubtedly heightened his emotional level. Thérèse was, to say the least, disheartened by her father's deteriorating condition, and, though she hoped he might be present when she took the veil in September, 1890, she knew it would not be possible. She wrote Céline:

> You know how immensely I longed to see our dearest father this morning; ah well! Now I see clearly that it is the good God's will that he should not be here. He allowed it simply to try our love.... Jesus wants me to be an orphan. He wants me to be alone with Him alone, that He may be united with me more intimately; and also He wants to give me, in the Homeland, the utterly legitimate joys He has refused me in the land of exile.[6]

Another sort of psychological suffering Thérèse endured was not at all unlike what many in religious life have known, the frequent cross of interpersonal relationships. True, Thérèse encountered this at an unusually young age, and the more spiritually mature one is the better one is able to cope. For a girl of fifteen, her maturity level was extraordinary.

> Yes, suffering opened wide its arms to me and I threw myself into them with love.... When one wishes to

---

[6] Thérèse to Céline, 23 September, 1890. Cited in F.J. Sheed (trans.), *Collected Letters of St. Thérèse of Lisieux* (New York: Sheed & Ward, 1949), 145.

attain a goal, one must use the means; Jesus made me understand that it was through suffering that He wanted to give me souls, and my attraction for suffering grew in proportion to its increase. This was my way for five years; exteriorly nothing revealed my suffering, which was all the more painful since I alone was aware of it.[7]

She is not referring to the rigors of Carmelite life, though she had good reason to — the little sleep, the curtailed diet, the loneliness, etc. It was, rather, the difficult personalities she had to contend with. The Lisieux Carmel in her time consisted of a community of twenty-six women of varying degrees of education, diverse personalities, age differences, health situations, and the like. Such living conditions do not always make for the most ideal tranquility, and Lisieux was no exception. Belgian Carmelite Conrad De Meester, in one of his profound studies on Thérèse, explains:

It is not always easy to live constantly with others in such close confinement. On the contrary: rubbing elbows with the same people and looking at the same faces day after day throughout a lifetime is scarcely enjoyable. To select only one of many possible instances, consider how very difficult Thérèse found the experience of trying to confide in her Mistress of Novices, Sister Marie des Anges. Although Sister Marie was sweet natured and always ready to offer good advice, Thérèse could not share the deepest aspirations of her soul with

[7] Clarke, op. cit., 149.

her, however hard she tried to do so. Then there was Sister Martha, one of Thérèse's novices, who was far from accommodating to begin with, and who seemed to enjoy opposing her at every turn. Her two sisters, Pauline and Marie, represented a trial of a different kind; Thérèse loved them dearly but neither wanted nor maintained a family relationship with them.[8]

Also to be considered was Thérèse's prioress for all but three years of her religious life (when Mother Agnes was prioress), Mother Marie de Gonzague. Thérèse grew very fond of her, and in many ways a close bond developed between the superior and the young sister. A deeply religious woman, Mother Gonzague could also be very temperamental at times, feeling somewhat threatened by so many of the Martin family in the community.

> Our Mother Prioress, frequently ill, had little time to spend with me. I know that she loved me very much and said everything good about me that was possible, nevertheless God permitted that she was VERY SE-VERE without her even being aware of it. I was unable to meet her without having to kiss the floor, and it was the same thing on those rare occasions when she gave me spiritual direction.[9]

After the fact, no one more convincingly witnessed to Thérèse's sanctity than Mother Marie de Gonzague, though day

---

[8] Conrad De Meester, OCD, *With Empty Hands: The Message of St. Thérèse of Lisieux* (London: Burns & Oates, A Continuum imprint, 2002), 25.

[9] Clarke, op. cit., 150.

to day reality during the young Saint's earthly life was somewhat different. On one occasion, Thérèse confided to a member of the community with whom she was close, that there had not been a single day of her Carmelite life without struggles and suffering.

The final type of trial Thérèse endured, certainly the most difficult, was physical — the tuberculosis that would ultimately claim her life. It was a suffering which began with her first coughing up blood on Good Friday, 1896, and did not conclude until her death on September 30, 1897. It must be considered in some detail to fully appreciate what she endured, and what she teaches modern men and women about such endurance.

From May until September, 1897, Thérèse suffered acutely at every level. The spiritual temptations against faith — namely faith in eternal life, were combined with the ravages of a disease that wore away her lungs and intestines. She became so emaciated, that some bones protruded through her skin. Fever, intense pain and difficulty in breathing were constant.

Abbé André Combes, one of the great Thérèsian scholars of some decades ago, saw an evolution in Thérèse's thoughts on suffering. She went from suffering as a joy, to suffering as union with Christ, to suffering for love alone, for the satisfaction of God's will alone. Thérèse expressed much of this in a letter to Céline:

> ...He is offering us a chalice as bitter as our feeble nature can bear. Let us not withdraw our lips from this chalice prepared by the hand of Jesus. Let us see life as it really is. It is a moment between two eternities. Let us suffer in peace. I admit that this word peace seemed a little strong to me, but the other day, when reflecting on it, I found the secret of suffering in peace. It is enough to will all that Jesus wills! To be the spouse

of Jesus we must resemble Jesus, and Jesus is all bloody.
He is crowned with thorns.[10]

Her thoughts sprang from a longtime devotion to the Holy
Face of Jesus, which was the second title she assumed in religious
life, following that of the Child Jesus. Thérèse's uncle, Isidore
Guerin, had a reproduction of the image of Our Lord's sacred
countenance as it has traditionally been depicted on Veronica's
Veil, placed in the Cathedral of Saint-Pierre in Lisieux, with a
perpetually lit oil lamp burning near it, maintained at his own
expense. This enkindled the young girl's devotion, and on April
26, 1885, she, along with her father and three sisters, was enrolled
in the Atoning Confraternity of the Holy Face, whose head-
quarters were located in Tours. This devotion had also been part
of the spiritual life of the Lisieux Carmel since the time of Mother
Genevieve of Saint Teresa, who encouraged each of the novices
to adopt it. Thérèse was introduced to this Carmel tradition by
her sister Pauline, who...

> showed her young sister that the disfigured face of the
> Saviour must encourage her to live in humility, to
> remain well hidden, and to become progressively the
> "enclosed garden" in which the Lord could take de-
> light, a "little Veronica" who would console Him.[11]

A poem Thérèse wrote expresses it even more poignantly:

> My joy is to love suffering
> I smile while shedding tears

---

[10] Thérèse to Céline, 4 April, 1889. Cited in O'Donnell, op. cit., 92.
[11] Pierre Descouvemont, *Thérèse and Lisieux* (Grand Rapids, MI: Wm. B. Eerdmans Publishing Co., 1996), 137.

I accept with gratitude
The thorns mingled with flowers....
If sometimes I shed tears
My joy is to hide them well
Oh! How many charms there are in suffering
When one knows how to hide it with flowers
I want only to suffer without saying so
So that Jesus may be consoled
My joy is to see Him smile
My joy is to struggle unceasingly
To bring forth spiritual children
It's with a heart burning with tenderness
That I keep saying to Jesus
I'm happy to suffer
My only joy on earth
Is to be able to please you[12]

On July 8, 1897, Thérèse was brought to the Carmel infirmary, where she would spend the remaining months of her life. From this point, she rarely was out of bed for more than two hours a day, and on days when she was coughing up significant amounts of blood, she remained in bed the entire day. Because of her condition, visits from the other sisters were kept to a strict minimum. The Virgin of the Smile, which had played such an important role in her early life, was placed close to her bed, and provided her great joy. July 27-28 was the beginning of what has been called the "great suffering." Now she actually began to speak of her physical sufferings; prior to this, they had been mere inconveniences! On July 30, she took a significant turn for the

---

[12] O'Donnell, op. cit., 94.

worse. She began suffocating, and was given medical assistance to breathe. At six o'clock in the evening, she was given the sacrament of Extreme Unction, and in the next room preparations were being made for her imminent burial. Such would not happen for two months, and in that time, she would give the world even more rich spirituality.

From the time she was first transferred to the infirmary until her death, Mother Agnes remained with Thérèse, during periods of recreation, while the community was reciting the Office, and at intervals when the infirmarians were needed elsewhere. Her sister was anxious that everything Thérèse said be retained, and she would hastily write each comment on loose sheets of paper. Eventually, they were recopied into a notebook. Thirty years later (1922-1923), she recopied these notes into a yellow leather-covered notebook; it has been known since as the "yellow notebook" of Mother Agnes. In 1927, this was published as the *Last Conversations*, and a great deal of its content involves the mystery of suffering. In early August, Thérèse had a respite from the intense pain she had been enduring, and was able to confide much to her sister. It was during this period also a picture of Theophane Venard was placed in the infirmary for her to see, so that she might pray to this young missionary. Venard was a member of the Society of the Foreign Missions, a French equivalent of what Maryknoll later became, a kindred soul on fire with the love of the Gospel, and its spread to foreign lands. Curiously, the picture of him in the infirmary has him pointing one finger in the direction of heaven, as if to indicate the happiness awaiting the struggling young Carmelite if she fought the good fight until the end.

By mid-August, Thérèse had reached the point of no return. Her left side became extremely painful, and her legs began to swell. The superior, Mother Marie de Gonzague realized a doctor's professional diagnosis was necessary, and she gave permission for Doctor Francis La Neele to examine her. La Neele was married to Isidore Guerin's daughter Jeanne, and by marriage, a cousin to Thérèse. He provided the only written diagnosis of her condition:

> "The right lung is completely gone, filled with tubercles in the process of softening. The lower third of the left lung is gone [...] the tuberculosis has reached the final stage." The word was finally uttered. The illness had invaded the entire body, including the intestines. The suffering was terrible. Thérèse was suffocating. They also feared an intestinal occlusion. "It's enough to make you lose your mind," she admitted, "Whenever I say: 'I am suffering,'" she said to Sister Genevieve, "you will answer: 'So much the better!' I don't have the strength, so you must finish what I would like to say."[13]

Three days after the diagnosis, Thérèse received Holy Communion for the last time. It was the feast of Saint Hyacinth, and she received for Father Hyacinthe Loyson, a very well known French Dominican who had left the priesthood, married, and begun what he called the French National Church.

On the infirmary wall, there was a fresco representing Christ in the Garden of Gethsemane accepting the chalice offered Him by an angel. Thérèse meditated on it over and over, seeing her own situation as the Lord undergoing in her the same agony. Her "great suffering" ended August 27th, her fever and congestion remained, and she could breathe with only half of her left lung. On August 30th, she was brought outside the cloister on a rolling bed as far

---

[13] Descouvement, op. cit., 298.

as the open door of the chapel, for her last visit to the Blessed Sacrament. The month of September saw the continued deterioration of her left lung, though she regained a certain interest in events around her, and responded whenever possible. A period of very intense agony began on the 29th. On the morning of the 30th, Sister Marie of the Sacred Heart quickly summoned Mother Agnes, who was sleeping in the cell off the cloister. Thérèse was gasping for breath, and could only utter the faintest of prayers to the Blessed Virgin. That afternoon, about two-thirty, she rallied somewhat, and was able to sit up in bed — something she had not been able to do for several weeks. Thirty minutes later, she stretched her arms out in the form of a cross, in an attempt to get some relief in breathing. The community had gathered in the infirmary, but left rather quickly, leaving only Mother Agnes with her. Her older sister later left this account:

> I was alone by her side. It was about half past four. Her face changed all of a sudden, and I understood it was her last agony. Mother Prioress returned and the whole community was soon assembled. She smiled but did not speak again until just before she died. For more than two hours, a terrible rattle tore her chest. Her face was flushed; her hands were purplish; she was trembling in all her members and her feet were as cold as ice. Large beads of perspiration stood out in drops on her forehead and ran down her cheeks. She was having more and more difficulty in breathing, and in order to breathe, she sometimes uttered little involuntary cries.[14]

---

[14] Guy Gaucher, *The Passion of Thérèse of Lisieux* (New York: Crossroad Publishing Company, 1998), 93.

Vivid as this depiction of her sufferings is, her death was quite peaceful. Mother Agnes continues…

> Her breathing suddenly became weaker and more labored. She fell back on the pillow, her head turned towards the right, the infirmary bell was rung and, to allow the nuns to assemble quickly, Mother Marie de Gonzague said in a loud voice: 'Open all the doors.' Hardly had the nuns knelt at her bedside when she pronounced very distinctly her final act of love: 'Oh! I love Him…' she said, looking at her crucifix. Then a moment later: 'My God, I… love you!' We thought that was the end, when, suddenly, she raised her eyes, eyes that were full of life, and shining with an indescribable happiness 'surpassing all her hopes.' Sister Marie of the Eucharist approached with a candle to get a better look at that sublime gaze which lasted for the space of a 'Credo.' The light from the candle passed back and forth in front of her eyes did not cause any movement in her eyelids…. It was twenty past seven.[15]

On Monday, October 4, 1897, Thérèse was the first Carmelite to be buried in a plot that had been purchased in the town cemetery for the community by Isidore Guerin. At the time of the purchase, he had not expected his niece would be the first Sister to be interred. Ironically, illness kept him from attending her funeral, though her sister Leonie, along with members of the Guerin and La Neele families led the mourners, in what was otherwise a nondescript funeral. A cult of devotion to the young

---

[15] Ibid., 94.

Sister began to spread quickly. And within six years, a young Scottish priest, who had cultivated a particularly strong devotion, suggested that the Lisieux Carmelites seriously look into the possibility of opening the cause for canonization. In September, 1910, the first official examination of her relics took place, and, after thirteen years, only her bones covered by shreds of cloth were discovered. She was then placed in a new casket, in a stone vault, where she remained until 1923. Today's pilgrim to Lisieux will find a large statue of the saint in the place where she rested for twenty-six years. In 1923, one month before her beatification, her relics were brought to the Carmel, to the reliquary where they remain to this day.

There was indeed a development in her understanding of suffering, but there is also a consistency. What she had learned as a child came to full maturity in Carmel. Her suffering had an element of detachment, a suffering endured for love alone, with complete confidence in the merciful love of God. For love alone meant, of course, bearing our crosses in union with Christ. When viewed in this way, the amount of suffering we are sent is of no consequence — it is our ability to associate it with the ongoing sufferings of our Redeemer, in His loving redemptive mission for mankind. Her strong message is that the graces we receive should not be hoarded for ourselves, but closely identified with the passion of Christ, who came to make possible our salvation. This is something that must be concretely done, and not merely spoken of. "It's very easy to write beautiful things about suffering," Thérèse said to Mother Agnes a few days before her death, "but writing is nothing, nothing! One must suffer in order to know!"[16]

---

[16] John Clarke, OCD, St. Thérèse of Lisieux: Her Last Conversations (Washington, DC: ICS Publications, 1977), 199-200.

Only those who have experienced the unrelenting pain of physical suffering can understand the slow undermining of a twenty-four year old body.... When Thérèse first became ill she was not unacquainted with suffering. But she was more familiar with moral suffering. The great trial of her life belonged to the past: the cerebral paralysis of her beloved father that had touched the innermost recesses of her being. Nothing could ever equal that abyss of sorrow into which she had been plunged at fifteen.... A person who comes through such a trial victorious at that age has matured.[17]

Thérèse teaches whatever the trials, problems, difficulties, or sufferings of our life, taken alone they are a waste; they are absolutely meaningless. Taken with Christ, they have the potential to bring us joy, or peace, or the uniting of our will with His, or all of these together. Wherever we are in our attitude toward suffering, we may learn a great deal from her.

Thérèse was very insistent that we not look back or forward. That, she said, is why people begin to despair. We are to live only in the present moment of grace the Lord has given us. We are never alone in our trials or problems — Christ is always with us.

...Let us profit from one moment of suffering. Let us see only one moment. A moment is a treasure. One act of love will make us know Jesus better...; it will bring us closer to Him during the whole of eternity.[18]

---

[17] Gaucher, op. cit. 97.
[18] Thérèse to Céline, 26 April, 1889. Cited in O'Donnell, op. cit., 98.

CHAPTER EIGHT

A SAINT FOR THE PESSIMIST

Over the great doors of the basilica in Lisieux, constructed through the generosity of Thérèse's devotees around the world, are found the words, *Ayez Confiance*, to have confidence — confidence in the merciful love of God. It is very difficult to take this message to heart and remain negative, no matter how long such thinking has prevailed in our lives. That is not to say temptations to discouragement will never come; such is unrealistic. What Thérèse offers, by contrast, is a true spiritual optimism — true, because it is so realistically grounded. On Trinity Sunday, 1895, with the permission of her superior, she made her Act of Oblation to the Merciful Love of God. In that beautiful offering of her life is to be found this thought:

> I am certain... that you will grant my desires; I know, O my God! That the more you want to give, the more you make us desire. I feel in my heart immense desires and it is with confidence I ask you to come and take possession of my soul.[1]

---

[1] John Clarke, OCD (trans.), *Story of a Soul: The Autobiography of Saint Thérèse of Lisieux* (Washington, DC: ICS Publications, 1996), 276.

Thérèse had come a long way in her own spiritual journey when she wrote those words, slightly more than two years before her death. It was a journey that began in childhood, when she acquired a confidence she never lost.

One of the earliest manifestations of it came in 1887, when she traveled on the pilgrimage from the diocese of Bayeux to Rome, to commemorate Pope Leo XIII's jubilee. While in the Eternal City, Thérèse and her sister Céline visited many of the holy sites pilgrims are wont to go, but one in particular made a great impression on her, the tomb of the early martyr Saint Cecilia. An entire morning spent in the catacombs seemed only a matter of minutes to the young girl. She and Céline managed to slip away from the group for awhile, to see the site of Cecilia's original burial, and later visited her house, transformed into a church. It is in the Trastevere section of Rome, adjacent to a cloistered convent of nuns. There, Thérèse learned that Cecilia had been designated patroness of music, not because she was gifted with a beautiful singing voice, nor because she was particularly adept at music, but because she had sung a hymn of virginal consecration to Our Lord as she walked to her death.

> Everything in her thrilled me, especially her abandonment, her limitless confidence that made her capable of virginizing souls who had never desired any other joys but those of the present life. St. Cecilia is like the bride in the Canticle; in her I see "a choir in an armed camp." Her life was nothing else but a melodious song in the midst of the greatest trials, and this does not surprise me because "the Gospel rested on her heart," and in her heart rested the Spouse of Virgins![2]

---

[2] Ibid., 131-132.

In Carmel, another episode highlights the young saint's confidence in God's mercy. It had to do with the influence of Mother Genevieve of Sainte Thérèse, saintly founder of the Lisieux Carmel, who had moved the community to their present home on Rue de Liverot, and who died some years after Thérèse's entrance into the community. Mother Genevieve had witnessed the beginning struggles of the community in Lisieux (after their arrival from Poitiers), and was, early on, elected Prioress. One of Thérèse's biographers described the elder nun as "a religious of consummate humility, who, by dint of application, had accustomed herself to carry out the ordinary duties of daily life with rare and supernatural perfection."[3] Her holiness was so pronounced, that Thérèse was compelled, at the moment of her death, to gather up her last tear, believing it to be the relic of a saint. Far greater was her spiritual impact on Thérèse.

> …[T]he memory Mother Genevieve left in my heart is a sacred memory. The day of her departure for heaven, I was particularly touched; it was the first time I had assisted at a death and really the spectacle was ravishing. I was placed at the foot of the dying Saint's bed, and witnessed her slightest movements. During the two hours I spent there, it seemed to me that my soul should have been filled with fervor; however, a sort of insensibility took control of me. But at the moment itself of our saintly Mother Genevieve's birth in heaven, my interior disposition changed, and in the twinkling of an eye I experienced an inexpressible joy and fervor; it was as though Mother Genevieve had imparted to

---

3 Msgr. August Laveille, *Life of the Little Flower: St. Thérèse of Lisieux* (New York: McMullen Books, 1953), 146.

me a little of the happiness she was enjoying, for I was convinced she went straight to heaven.[4]

In fact, some of this spiritual confidence had preceded Mother Genevieve's death. Two months earlier, the community had made its annual retreat under Father Alexis Prou, a Franciscan recollect from Caen. He was superior of the house of St. Lazaire, and during the course of his conferences, Thérèse admitted to receiving great graces. She noted that oftentimes, preached retreats caused her more pain than the ones she made alone, but this particular year, she had made a preparatory novena with great intensity. Curiously, she was experiencing great interior temptations about the existence of heaven as early as 1891, and was much in need of spiritual solace.

> I felt disposed to say nothing of my interior dispositions since I didn't know how to express them, but I had hardly entered the confessional when I felt my soul expand. After speaking only a few words, I was understood in a marvelous way and my soul was like a book in which this priest read better than I did myself. He launched me full sail upon the ways of confidence and love which so strongly attracted me, but upon which I dared not advance. He told me that my faults caused God no pain, and that holding as he did God's place he was telling me in His name that God was very much pleased with me.
>
> Oh! How happy I was to hear those consoling words! Never had I heard that our faults could not

---

[4] Clarke, op. cit., 170.

cause God any pain, and this assurance filled me with joy, helping me to bear patiently with life's exile.[5]

One of Thérèse's major concerns was her sister Céline. She was the last Martin sister to remain in the world, and had spent considerable time caring for her father. Céline was an unusually beautiful girl, and had a number of male suitors. Though she always felt the strong attraction to Carmel, she could not tell, with complete assurance, which path in life God had chosen for her. Thérèse, on the other hand, was absolutely convinced of her older sister's religious vocation, and prayed unceasingly that Céline would join her in Carmel — not because she wanted her sister with her for human support, since too much human dependence would have lessened her ability to concentrate on the God she loved so much. Rather, it was her complete conviction that Céline was called to the same sort of life as herself.

> Since my entrance into Carmel I can say that my affection for Céline was a mother's love rather than a sister's. When she was to attend a party one day, the very thought of it caused me so much pain that I begged God to prevent her from dancing and (contrary to my custom) I even shed a torrent of tears. Jesus deigned to answer me. He permitted that His little fiancée be unable to dance that evening (even though she was not embarrassed to dance gracefully when it was necessary). She was invited to dance and was unable to refuse the invitation, but her partner found out he was totally powerless to make her dance; to his great confusion he was condemned simply to walking in order to conduct

---

[5] Ibid., 173-174.

her to her place, and then he made his escape and did not reappear for the whole evening. This incident, unique in its kind, made me grow in confidence and love for the One who set His seal upon my forehead and had imprinted it at the same time upon that of my dear Céline.[6]

This rather humorous event took place at the wedding of Henri Maudelonde, a nephew of the Guerins. It was one of many which increased Thérèse's ever-growing sense of confidence in God's merciful love, making it all the easier for her, eventually, to conclude the heart of her autobiography, Manuscript B, saying...

O Jesus! Why can't I tell all little souls how unspeakable is your condescension? I feel that if You found a soul weaker and littler than mine, which is impossible, You would be pleased to grant it still greater favors, provided it abandoned itself with total confidence to Your infinite Mercy. But why do I desire to communicate Your secrets of love, O Jesus, for was it not You alone who taught them to me, and can You not reveal them to others? Yes, I know it, and I beg You to do it. I beg You to cast Your Divine Glance upon a great number of little souls. I beg You to choose a legion of little Victims worthy of Your LOVE![7]

It was her constant meditation on the mysteries of faith that revealed to Saint Thérèse even more directly the depths of this

---

[6] Ibid., 176-177.
[7] Ibid., 200.

mystery. All the salvific events of the life of Christ were simply manifestations of God's mercy toward His weak, helpless children. The way of spiritual childhood, the way of supreme confidence of Thérèse is something the world often smiles at, though in fact, countless souls have often been unexpectedly changed by it, when nothing else worked. One who easily falls into this category is her first priest brother, Maurice Bellière.

Bellière had written to Mother Agnes in October, 1895, much in need of a very spiritual sister with whom to correspond. He had mentioned to the Prioress that years earlier he had committed a great blunder which he much regretted. One could speculate endlessly about particulars, but what concerned Mother Agnes the most was finding the appropriate correspondent to help a priest in his spiritual brokenness. Since the death of their mother in 1877, Pauline had become mother to Thérèse, and perhaps no one knew the young woman's spiritual depth with more intimacy. It was, therefore, no partiality to her sister that caused the Prioress to assign Thérèse to Father Bellière; it was a deep seated conviction she could do him the most spiritual good.

Maurice Bellière was born in Caen in 1874, and raised by an aunt and uncle from the time he was just a few weeks old. His mother had died one week after his birth, and his father, after depositing him with his relatives, promptly vanished from his life. Young Bellière was eleven years old when finally told the true story. As a young man, he felt a call to the priesthood and applied to the Foreign Mission Society. There was some question about his academic ability — especially in philosophy and theology, two disciplines very important in priestly studies. There was also some concern about his adaptability to life in the Foreign Missions. He next chose the diocesan priesthood, but was held up on his reception of the Minor Order of Tonsure, a sign, in those days, that there were serious things about the individual which had to be corrected if he were expecting to continue in the seminary. Finally, with some priestly support, Maurice applied to the Society of the African Missions, more popularly called the White Fathers, from their white habit. He was accepted, finally, and would spend some years with them before dying at a young age. His career was anything but laudatory, though he was given the extraordinary grace of corresponding with a saint.

A series of twenty-one letters would be exchanged between the two, and these missives have been the subject of a serious study by New York's Auxiliary Bishop, Patrick V. Ahern. Of the twenty-one, two in particular stress the confidence the young nun wanted to instill in Maurice. In his first letter to Thérèse, he signed himself "Your miserable brother," a sure sign she had her work cut out for her. She responded by assuring him she was doing everything possible to secure the necessary graces he requested. At the same time, she let him know that the only real happiness or joy we will feel in this life is doing the will of God — especially if His will entailed suffering. It was a beautiful lot Father Bellière had in life, since it closely resembled what Christ Himself had endured. In the course of her letter, Thérèse quotes from Père Almire Pichon, a Jesuit friend of the Martin family and spiritual director to the Martin sisters. He went to Canada to preach missions and retreats, and through the years Thérèse wrote over one hundred letters to him, all of which he destroyed, for reasons of confidentiality. Thérèse once said that her entire soul had been poured into one specific letter. She hoped the advice offered her by her friend Pichon might be of help to Bellière.

A Saint has said "the greatest honor that God can pay to anyone is not to give him much but to ask much from him...." He wants you to begin your mission already and to save souls through suffering. Isn't it by suffering and dying that He Himself redeemed the world? I know that you aspire to the joy of laying down your life for the divine Master, but martyrdom of the heart is no less fruitful than that of bloodshed.[8]

Thérèse's letter of July 26, 1897, written in the midst of excruciating pain just two months before her death, is once again written to a forlorn soul — one who was deeply troubled by past infidelities. She began by reminding him of the doctrine of the Communion of Saints, and especially of how much more value she would be to him after she left this world. In this, she was merely reflecting on the intimacy existing between the church triumphant in heaven, the church suffering anticipated love in purgatory, and the church militant, those who still make their pilgrim journey through this world, and how the sharing of spiritual goods is the most priceless thing we can do, one for another. In reading the letter, one sees clearly Thérèse wishes to secure for Maurice the same sort of confidence she has acquired in her own life.

> He has forgiven your infidelities long ago. Only your desires for perfection remain to make His heart rejoice. I implore you; don't drag yourself to His feet ever again. Follow that "first impulse which draws you into His arms...." I completely agree with you that "the heart of God is saddened more by the thousand little indelicacies of His friends than it is by the faults, even by

---

[8] Thérèse to Maurice Bellière, December 26, 1896, cited in Patrick V. Ahern, *Maurice and Thérèse: The Story of a Love* (New York: Doubleday, 1998), 64.

the grave ones, which people of the world commit."
But my dear little brother, it seems to me that it is only
when His friends, ignoring their continual indelicacies,
make a habit out of them and don't ask forgiveness for
them, that Jesus can utter those touching words which
the church puts on His lips in Holy Week: "These
wounds you see in the palms of my hands are the ones
I received in the house of those who loved me." For
those who love Him, and after each fault come to ask
pardon by throwing themselves into His arms, Jesus
trembles with joy.[9]

One can feel so strongly the optimism and spiritual
confidence flowing from her pen, and one can only hope and
pray it helped Bellière, who eventually left the White Fathers,
returned to his native France, displayed much erratic behavior
(later discovered to result from a poisonous bite he received from
an African insect, which slowly worked its way into his blood
stream), and died shortly thereafter. His tombstone in Langrune
today reads "Spiritual Brother and protégé to Saint Thérèse."
Bishop Ahern notes that...

> Maurice was that quintessential "little soul" to whom
> Thérèse was attracted, the prototype of most of us.
> He deserves our attention for that very reason — not
> because he was great but because he was not. Millions
> of people in the century since her death have been
> drawn to Thérèse and want to know more about her.
> Almost all of them are ordinary. She is the friendliest

---

[9] Thérèse to Maurice Bellière, July 26, 1897, cited in ibid., 189.

of saints, in whose company an ordinary person feels at home. She... uncovers and appeals to the mystic that lies within every human being. She makes the quest for holiness easy, in the sense that she makes clear that God asks of us no more than we can give. She does not try to force high standards on us. She draws us, asking only that we trust in the God who is "nothing but mercy and love."[10]

It is that same kind of spiritual kinship she offers to everyone who takes her teaching to heart. It can happen individually, and it can happen collectively. Proof that the message of spiritual childhood, the promise Thérèse made of spending her heaven doing good on earth was being daily fulfilled, not just in individual lives, but among thousands will be found very convincingly in our own twenty-first century. Her relics began traveling the world, and the spiritual results were little short of astounding. A good case in point is the Republic of Ireland, where they visited from April 15 through June 28, 2001. Ireland has traditionally been thought of as a Catholic country, in fact a staunchly Catholic one. This has not been exaggerated, though in the late twentieth and early twenty-first centuries, Ireland has not escaped the spiritual malaise of the rest of Western Europe: declining birth rates, calls for liberalization of the nation's abortion laws, sexual promiscuity, a decline in Mass attendance, a significant drop in the number of priestly and religious vocations, Catholic politicians quite vocally at variance with church moral teachings, and the like. Into this scene came the relics of Thérèse, drawing one-third of the nation's population of four million. Seventy-five thousand people came through Saint

---

[10] Ibid., 281-282.

Mary's Pro-Cathedral in Dublin when the relics first arrived in the nation's capital. There were to be one hundred fifteen stops at churches throughout the country, keeping a schedule of two hours traveling, and twenty-two hours spent at given churches. Churches remained open all night, with lines sometimes one-half mile long. Moving throughout the country, there were many small churches not scheduled for a stop, but the local priest, along with two to three hundred people, would be lined up along the route the "Thérèse-mobile" would be traveling, and the motorcade would naturally stop and allow the local townspeople to venerate the relics. One prominent Irish Carmelite, Father Joseph Linus Ryan, O.Carm., a former Provincial of the Carmelites in Ireland, and national coordinator of the visit, stated in one Irish newspaper that the visit was the "greatest mass movement of our people in history," and he was quick to add there was no superficiality in the people's devotion. Lines for confession were little less than extraordinary, given the modern predicament, and priests around the country could not get over the number of penitents who had been away from the sacrament for ten to twenty years returning. Such statistics are not exaggerations; they are hard, cold facts, presenting any believer a great deal of difficulty remaining in the spiritual doldrums of pessimism!

So the spirit of childhood taught by Thérèse attracts many, and yet there are others who remain aloof from it, thinking that by staying aloof they are very prudently keeping themselves from becoming overtly sentimental. What they are missing is the regrettable part.

An objection often raised, and validly so, is this: Thérèse concentrates so much on the merciful love of God, is it not possible that she forgets about the justice of God? One Thérèse scholar has answered the question very well:

…To think this would indicate a wrong understanding of the relationship between God's mercy and His justice. He is merciful because He is just.… True justice takes into account good intentions, the circumstances which lessen the responsibility no less than those which increase it. God makes allowance for weakness and failings as we rarely do — we are neither just nor merciful enough, because we do not realize our own weaknesses and so do not make allowances for the weakness of others; but God sees us as we really are, and before punishing us, in justice, He begins by considering our profound misery; His justice excites His mercy. Now Saint Thérèse, because she was so conscious of her weakness, saw this truth so clearly that the thought of God's justice, far from terrifying her, only added to her confidence and joy.[11]

She beautifully describes this confidence and joy:

Since it has been given to me to understand the love of the heart of Jesus, I confess that all fear has been driven from mine. The remembrance of my faults humbles me and helps me never to rely on my own strength which is mere weakness. Still more does that remembrance speak to me of mercy and love. When with childlike confidence we cast our faults into Love's all devouring furnace, how can they fail to be utterly consumed?[12]

[11] Vernon Johnson, *Spiritual Childhood: The Spirituality of St. Thérèse of Lisieux* (San Francisco: Ignatius Press, 2001), 94.

[12] *Spirit of St. Thérèse*. Comp. by the Carmelites of Lisieux (Burns and Oates), 179, cited in ibid., 103.

It is true that many hardened sinners have returned to the path of grace through Thérèse's intercession. But so often, those who follow her devoutly are not hardened sinners; rather, they are holy people who are desirous of becoming holier. And it is in this genuine desire that so many of us fail each day. Why? Because of our weakened human nature — the result of Original Sin in all of us. These daily falls cause many to lose confidence, despair of the heights of sanctity, and settle into a mediocre spirituality. Saint Thérèse has been sent to reawaken in all of us the confidence we need so badly. She does it by telling us of the fatherhood of God, and our total dependence on that fatherhood.

Thérèse was absolutely convinced she was destined to be a great saint, not from any sort of arrogance on her part, but because she had meditated so long and hard on the words of Scripture, she had loved the Lord in the Eucharist, she had constant recourse to the Blessed Mother — all the components of sanctity, and she tells each of us we can be the same, we can follow her on the path to sanctity. Her many words written in *The Story of a Soul* and elsewhere are not merely the outpourings of a great saint with no meaning for us. They were written with us in mind — with every "little soul" in the world in mind, excluding only those who felt they were too spiritually advanced — and most people in that category would be presumptuous indeed. Every sentence in her magnificent autobiography has something for us, if we will but read it slowly, prayerfully, and take it very personally to heart. To the extent we do, we will begin to trust in Our Lord's promises, and see our very weaknesses and failings as the surest means at our disposal to run into the arms of His loving mercy and forgiveness.

CHAPTER NINE

THÉRÈSE ON THE PRIESTHOOD AND THE HOLY EUCHARIST

Monsignor Vernon Johnson's story is a very interesting one. He was born into a well-to-do English family in 1886, and as a young man felt a calling to the Anglican ministry. In 1910, he became a minister of that church, and was first assigned to the coastal town of Brighton, a relatively short distance from London. He remained in that assignment for three years, all the while longing for the more intense discipline of a religious congregation. In 1914, he entered the Anglo-Catholic Society of Divine Compassion, a community that wore the Franciscan habit. Along with fellow monks, he opened Saint Giles, a home for the small number of London's lepers, much in need of living out their final days in dignity and peace.

Sometime after the home's establishment, he went to London's east end to work with the poor. These were the years of the First World War, and since there was no shelter to escape air raids on the east end, Johnson and his companions would often go to individual families who were only too happy to offer shelter. The monks had been living in a small monastery in the east end, and when the raids were over, they returned to find the structure demolished — only a crucifix remained.

Johnson served in a number of Anglican houses of his order after the war, being sought after as a retreat master. In 1924, while making his own private retreat in a religious house, an Anglican nun offered him a copy of *The Story of a Soul* for his spiritual reading. He thanked the sister very kindly, but said he was little interested, since the story was both French and Roman Catholic. The nun, not to be outdone, told him he should not entertain such prejudices, and the book's contents might do him the world of good. After reading part of Manuscript A, he felt the young writer was "a pious little prig."[1] Something made him continue, and only then did Thérèse begin to emerge. He could not stop reading; it moved him as no other book had. He became so intrigued he went to France, to Lisieux, to Les Buissonets, and, once at her home he had no need of a guide — he had read Thérèse's autobiography so well, and so many times, each room in the home followed in perfect order.

The beautiful garden at Les Buissonets particularly fascinated him, and he became so engrossed with his surroundings, he paid no attention to the fact that he and others had been locked in for the evening! At least he had opportunity to converse with a very interesting Belgian priest, and when he returned to his lodgings for dinner, his tardiness proved beneficial; he was seated with a fellow pilgrim who suggested that after dinner, the two take a walk to the cemetery where Thérèse's parents are buried. While there, he chanced to meet one of Thérèse's classmates who took an interest in the Anglican divine, and arranged for him to meet Mother Agnes the following morning in the parlor of the Carmel. Years later, he would write:

---

[1]   Sister Marie Immanuel, SC, "How St. Thérèse Found a Priest Brother" in Vernon Johnson, *Spiritual Childhood: The Spirituality of St. Thérèse of Lisieux* (San Francisco: Ignatius Press, 2001), 223.

I was conscious that my visit was being guided in a mysterious way. At first it seemed coincidence... but as time went on I knew it was more than mere coincidence which led me, a stranger, and an unknown, to kneel in the Carmel parlor and receive the blessing of Mother Agnes, the Saint's own sister; I must believe it was the prayers of the little Saint herself.[2]

Within a year, he returned to Lisieux and had to confront the haunting question of his future; was a Church which produced such an extraordinary young woman, in fact, the true Church? Very likely he had answered in the affirmative, but did not want to admit it to himself. In his prayers, he sincerely entreated the Lord not to ask such a sacrifice of him — giving up the religious heritage so precious to him all his life. Three years later, that is exactly what he did. It was not long after his reception into the Catholic Church, that he knew he was called to be a priest. Vernon found himself off to Rome, to study at the Beda, an English Seminary for older vocations, located near the famous basilica of Saint Paul's Outside the Walls. At age forty-nine he returned to England for ordination, and within two weeks was back in Lisieux to offer Mass for the sisters in the Carmel who had prayed so constantly for his perseverance. Appropriately, during the Mass, he used the chalice Thérèse had so often prepared for other priests' use while she served as sacristan.

What Father Johnson did for and with Saint Thérèse in his three happy decades in the Catholic priesthood makes another story, for he dedicated his life to

---

[2] Ibid., 226.

spreading her Little Way, especially carrying on her apostolate to priests, organizing the Association of the Priests of Saint Thérèse, editing *Sicut Parvuli*, a quarterly review for the associates, and spending himself in giving retreats and days of recollection steeped in the Thérèsian theology so geared to priestly needs.... Mindful to the last of St. Thérèse's desire to bring priests closer to Christ, he said wistfully to his nurse just before he died, "Sister, I don't feel that I've done as much as I should have for priests." She reassured him, and he smiled and said, "Thank you, Sister! Now I am very happy." Those were his last words. He died in 1969 at the age of eighty. Thérèse's protégé had used well the roses she had showered down on him for so many years![3]

Why would Monsignor Johnson so tirelessly spend his priestly energy spreading the message of the Little Way? It was not simply because Thérèse's message had made such an impact on him; after all, lay people all over the world could claim the same reaction. It was, rather, the intimacy Saint Thérèse has with priests, clearly expressed during her canonical examination prior to entering Carmel. Her response to why she felt called to such a life has become famous: "I came to save souls and especially to pray for priests."[4]

But why, specifically, pray for priests? One could argue that coming from a family of such conspicuous Catholic piety, the priesthood was held in great awe; and without a doubt, a strong

---

[3] Ibid., 229-230.

[4] John Clarke, OCD (trans), *Story of a Soul: The Autobiography of Saint Thérèse of Lisieux* (Washington, DC: ICS Publications 1996), 149.

case could be made for it. It was more the humanity of priests, however, which made her realize that such men, though set apart by God, were also weak, fallible, indeed, sinful. This became very clear to her as a young girl when she traveled on the diocesan pilgrimage to Rome for the jubilee of Pope Leo XIII. There were several priests in the group, and, in some instances, their conduct was less than edifying.

> I understood my vocation in Italy and that's not going too far in search of such useful knowledge. I lived in the company of many saintly priests for a month and I learned that, though their dignity raises them above the angels, they are nevertheless weak and fragile men. If holy priests, whom Jesus in the gospel calls the "salt of the earth," show in their conduct their extreme need for prayers, what is to be said of those who are tepid? Didn't Jesus say too: "If the salt loses its savor, where-with will it be salted?" How beautiful is the vocation, O Mother, which has as its aim the preservation of the salt destined for souls! This is Carmel's vocation since the sole purpose of our prayers and sacrifices is to be the apostle of the apostles. We are to pray for them while they are preaching to souls through their words and especially their example. I must stop here, for were I to continue I would never come to an end![5]

Small wonder Thérèse's work in the sacristy had such great appeal for her.... She worked there from 1891 until 1893, and returned again in March, 1896, to work with her cousin Marie

---

[5] Ibid. 122.

Guerin, Sister Marie of the Eucharist. There is a famous photograph of Thérèse with her three sisters and their cousin taken in the sacristy courtyard. It depicts Mother Agnes, Sister Marie of the Sacred Heart, and Sister Genevieve preparing the Eucharistic bread — they were bakers, a lucrative work for many convents in the nineteenth century. Sister Marie of the Eucharist appears to be pouring altar wine into a cruet, while Thérèse is filling a ciborium with hosts, a priestly act oftentimes, but one for which she drew the comparison of "filling heaven" by the spiritual apostolate of prayer.

In November, 1896, she composed a verse titled "The Sacristans of Carmel" which she dedicated to Sister Marie Philoméne, with whom she had been in the Novitiate, and who now worked with her in the sacristy.

> Our happiness and our glory
> is to work for Jesus.
> His beautiful heaven
> is the ciborium
> we want to fill with the elect.[6]

Thérèse had known only one bishop, Bishop Hugonin, with whom she dealt in trying to secure permission to enter Carmel. She had known a number of priests, and undoubtedly disclosed more of her spiritual life to Almire Pichon, the French Jesuit who ultimately went to Canada as a missionary, than to any other priest. She also knew Abbé Youf, the chaplain of the Carmel, who had assumed his position in 1873, and would remain there

---

[6] Pierre Descouvemont, *Thérèse and Lisieux* (Grand Rapids, MI: Wm. B. Eerdmans Publishing Co. 1996), 176.

twenty-four years, dying just eight days after Thérèse's own death, in 1897. Youf was a hard worker, constantly reading books on spirituality to aid him in his work of giving spiritual conferences to the community. His health was very fragile, and parish work, as then constituted, was thought too taxing for him. Through her visits to Carmel, Thérèse had gotten to know him long before her own entry, and she never forgot the advice he gave her to seek permission to enter the convent as soon as she reached her fifteenth birthday.

> Thérèse had great affection for him. In her opinion he was "the priest," the one who received the power to consecrate the Body of Christ and to hold it in his hands. With what love she prepared the sacred vessels in the sacristy! With what care she painted and illumined the missal he used at the altar. He was Thérèse's regular confessor though she did not experience the great wave of confidence as with Father Alexis Prou. Thérèse understood early that Jesus wanted to be her only "director."[7]

Some proponents of women's ordination have tried to see in Thérèse a hero, one ahead of her time, because she so admired that unique configuration to Christ, and felt within herself the "vocation of Warrior, Priest, Apostle, Doctor and Martyr."[8] In fact, her appreciation for Christ's priesthood is what kept her from aspiring to the same, even in her mind. "Though I desire to be a priest," she wrote, "I admire and envy the humility of Saint

---

[7] Ibid., 260.
[8] Ibid., 272.

Francis of Assisi and I sense in myself the call to imitate him by refusing the sublime dignity of the priesthood."[9]

It was as spiritual confidant to priests that Thérèse would excel. In May, 1896, Maurice Bellière was joined by Adoph Roulland, Thérèse's second spiritual brother. He had been born at Cahagnolles in the Calvados region in 1870, first studied for the diocesan priesthood, and later entered the Foreign Mission Society at Paris, where he was ordained in June, 1896. A few days later, he offered Mass in the chapel of the Lisieux Carmel, and met with Mother Marie de Gonzague and Thérèse in the parlor. Roulland had previously written to the Prioress, asking for the spiritual assistance of a sister correspondent. Mother Gonzague thought of Thérèse immediately, but at first, the young sister was a bit reluctant to take on yet another priest brother, feeling her own lack of confidence. Out of obedience, she not only accepted, but also began the friendship by hand painting a pall for Father Roulland to use at Mass. This she presented as a gift the day of his visit, and a series of six letters ensued between the two before the saint's death. The young missionary eventually left Marseilles by boat bound for China. Prior to his departure, his Carmelite sister had penned a poem for him, which she dedicated "To Our Lady of Victories, Queen of Virgins, Apostles and Martyrs," the first two stanzas of which are telling:

> To Missionary work forever
> You united me above
> By the bonds of prayer
> Of suffering and of love
> He to cross the earth is given

---

[9] Ibid., 273.

> Preaching the name of Jesus
> I in shadow all hidden
> Do practice humble virtues[10]

Five days before his ordination, Thérèse had written to Father Roulland, assuring him that she would be happy "to work with you for the salvation of souls," adding "it is for this purpose that I became a Carmelite nun; being unable to be an active missionary, I wanted to be one through love and penance."[11] Within days of his departure for the Orient, Thérèse reassured him he would never be far from her thoughts or prayers:

> ...I have attached the map of Su-Tchuen on the wall where I work, and the picture you gave me is resting always on my heart in the book of the Gospels which never leaves me... distance will never be able to separate our souls, death itself will make our union more intimate. If I go to heaven soon, I will ask Jesus' permission to go to visit you at Su-Tchuen, and we shall continue our apostolate together.[12]

It was because of contacts such as these that the Union of Priests of St. Thérèse of the Child Jesus was begun on March 29, 1929, in the chapel of the Carmel of Lisieux. Since that day, thousands of priests have become members. Less than five years after its foundation, one Thérèsian priest explained its importance:

[10] "Introduction to the Correspondence of Sister Thérèse of the Child Jesus and the Holy Face and Father Adolphe Roulland (1870-1934)" in *Union Sacerdotale de Sainte Thérèse de Lisieux* (Lisieux: Direction du Pelerinage de Lisieux, Juin, 1998), 68.

[11] Ibid., 70.

[12] Thérèse to Adolph Roulland, July 30, 1896. Cited in *Union Sacerdotale de Sainte Th' de Lisieux* (Lisieux: Direction du Pelerinage de Lisieux, October, 1998), 49-51.

The place of the priests of the Confraternity of St. Thérèse is in the forefront of the battle; they must sacrifice themselves to the full, cast aside all human wisdom and take the sword of the Spirit which is the word of God by which they will vanquish all the might of the Adversary.[13]

Such was all the more necessary, given the world of the early 1930's.

The world which they must encounter [i.e. priests ordained in the early 30's] differs in the most fundamental manner from that which we have faced; we have seen the beginning of the revolt, they must face it in all its fury. Hitherto when men sinned they recognized it as sin and never for a moment pretended it was virtue. There have been great sinners in the past but they never posed as great saints.... But the neo-Pagan of today indulges lust and sensual passion to the full and calls it virtue. The whole difference between the old world and the new lies here.[14]

An interesting commentary on the pre-Second World War world, which might well be applied to our own times; nonetheless, the importance of apostolic work on the part of priests dedicated to Thérèse is what is paramount. The priest author who saw the vital need for priests to keep close to Thérèse's Little Way was himself no exception.

---

[13] Benedict Williamson, *The Doctrinal Mission and Apostolate of St. Thérèse of Lisieux, Volume I: The Priesthood* (London: Alexander Ouseley Limited, 1932), 8.

[14] Ibid., 4-5.

Throughout the years of my priestly ministry my saintly mistress has been with me and I have always had the sense of her presence; in moments of exceptional peril she directly intervened, in all the difficulties of my spiritual life, in all my work for souls she has always been at hand to guide and direct, and in moments of distress and discouragement to comfort and console.

The more I have studied and striven to enter into the meaning of her doctrine, and put into practice all she has taught me, the more I have realized how her way of love and abandon responds to every need of the human soul; indeed I cannot think what my life would have been without her to guide and enlighten me.[15]

Seven decades later, a priest in Indiana was to write similar thoughts of gratitude. He described his life growing up, the pranks he was inclined to play on people — pranks which had a humorous and not so humorous side to them, and, in particular, how his mother once told him of Thérèse, and encouraged him to offer all the little things of life to God. This struck him as a very realistic approach in his own life, because he was not yet prepared to offer anything greater. He grew in his appreciation for Thérèse's human side, noting that she, too, played pranks on her fellow members of the community! In any event, this young man's very Catholic background compelled him to love the church and the priestly life — so much so he applied for and was accepted to study for the diocesan priesthood.

From the beginning of my days in the seminary I went to St. Thérèse and entrusted my vocation to her. There

---

was a statue not far from the seminary. Every September 30, the anniversary of her death, I decorated the marble flowers in her arms with the petals of roses and marigolds. Her *Story of a Soul* became my spiritual guide, and I, very imperfectly, did my best to follow. My spiritual director at the time poked a little fun at this devotion, calling it sentimental, but I remember thinking that surrender to Love was never sentimental, that in fact it required great strength and was something we could not do alone. I enlisted St. Thérèse to help me. She must have grown frustrated with me at times! In her *Last Conversations* I loved her complete abandonment and asked God to help me follow this "sure way" of spiritual childhood.

I am certain that the prayers and love of the Little Flower brought me to ordination.... I have read everything I can get my hands on about her.... To this day, Thérèse and I continue our conversations and her little way of spiritual childhood brings me such joy. One day we will meet in the Homeland, and I will thank her face to face for leading me to know and cleave to Love Himself. I can hardly wait![16]

It is because of testimonies such as these that the Sacerdotal Union of St. Thérèse exists at Lisieux. In her, priests have found a "little sister" who knows how to understand them and assist them in their mission. Many priest members are likewise very conscious of the voice of the Church, which has acknowledged the value of her teaching and entrusted to her the missions of the

---

[16] "Saint Thérèse and My Vocation," in Elizabeth Ficocelli, *Shower of Heavenly Roses* (New York: The Crossroad Publishing Company, 2004), 196.

entire world. The Union does not impose a detailed way of life on its members; rather, its only aim is to promote the spirit of the Gospel as it was lived by Saint Thérèse. It keeps before all priest members' minds the saint who was filled with the action of the Holy Spirit, and the life of the Blessed Trinity, and called to live a life of love for the least of Our Lord's followers, especially those who feel themselves worthless. A plenary indulgence is granted to each member on the day of his entry into the Association, and also each year on the feast of Saint Thérèse of the Child Jesus, October 1st. In order that the canonical status of the Union be in conformity with the norms of the New Code of Canon Law, promulgated in 1983, it has been raised to a Private Association of the Faithful, and opened to Permanent Deacons.

Such an organization can only bring consolation to priests, those uniquely configured to Christ, for whom Thérèse felt such deep spiritual affection. For her who felt prayer to be an aspiration of the heart, and was given to much spontaneity in her conversation with God, it is all the more significant that each day of her Carmelite life she prayed this prayer for priests:

O Holy Father, may the torrents of love flowing from the sacred wounds of Thy divine Son bring forth priests like unto the beloved disciple John who stood at the foot of the Cross; priests who as a pledge of Thine own most tender love will lovingly give Thy Divine Son to the souls of men.

May Thy priests be faithful guardians of Thy church, as John was of Mary, whom he received into his house. Taught by this loving mother who suffered so much on Calvary, may they display a mother's care and thoughtfulness towards Thy children. May they teach souls to enter into close union with Thee through Mary, who, as the Gate of Heaven, is specially the guardian of the treasurers of Thy Divine Heart.

Give us priests who are on fire, and who are true children of Mary, priests who will give Jesus to souls with the same tenderness and care with which Mary carried the Little Child of Bethlehem.

Mother of sorrows and of love, out of compassion for thy beloved Son, open in our hearts deep wells of love, so that we may console Him and give Him a generation of priests formed in thy school and having all the tender thoughtfulness of thine own spotless love.[17]

In her time, Saint Thérèse knew, perhaps with greater intensity and appreciation than many modern believers of the twenty-first century, that, without the priesthood, there can be no gift of the Holy Eucharist; indeed, the Eucharist is the raison d'être of the priesthood. For this reason, Thérèse, in her love and admiration for priests, must be considered a very Eucharistic saint as well. Father Stéphane Piat, the Franciscan who wrote *The Story of a Family* decades ago, referred to Thérèse as the "Saint of the Eucharist," and for very valid reasons. The photograph of her as Carmel sacristan shows her love of the Eucharist as much as it does her love of the Priesthood. She expressed many times the great joy she experienced preparing the vessels in which the Body and Blood of Our Lord would rest. It was that sort of love which, no doubt, motivated her to write...

17 Fr. J. Linus Ryan, O.Carm. "Saint Thérèse 'Sister and Friend' of Priests," in *Celebrating the First Anniversary-St. Thérèse Relics Irish Visit 2001* (Dublin: St. Thérèse National Office, Terenure College, Spring, 2002), 15.

> Thy spouse am I. Thy chosen one
> My well-beloved; Come dwell in me.
> Oh come! Thy beauty wins my heart
> Deign to transform me into Thee.[18]

Thérèse was raised in a Eucharistic family. Her parents, Zélie and Louis Martin, attended daily Mass at five-thirty each morning in the parish church in Alençon, a custom her father kept up after moving to Lisieux. Both her parents went to Holy Communion as often as was then permitted, and, in her early childhood years in Lisieux, Thérèse would accompany her father on daily visits to the town's churches to spend time with Our Lord in the Blessed Sacrament. By the time she was old enough to enroll in the Benedictine school in Lisieux, she would go to the chapel each afternoon at one-thirty and spend one quarter hour with the Lord. Even then, her companions later noted, she gave the appearance of one who was deeply lost in contemplation. Her friendship with Christ had deepened to a remarkable degree by the time she made her First Holy Communion.

> The day of her First Communion was an experience of pure spiritual bliss without shadow or disturbance. The piety of the time, remote as it was from the Liturgy, understood Communion, and especially First Communion, as something almost apart from the Mystery of the Mass, exclusively as a ceremony of meeting (in fact of "wedding" as the devotional books were wont to say) of the individual soul with the Saviour within the sacrament. Thérèse's experience was in terms of

---

[18] Cited in Fr. Stéphane Jos. Piat, OFM, "Saint of the Eucharist," in *St. Thérèse: Doctor of the Little Way* (New Bedford, MA: Franciscan Friars of the Immaculate, 1997), 150.

this pattern, but she drew from the stereotype its fullest content. The child experienced all the emotional storm and rapture of passionate surrender, of a true union with God. In retrospect Thérèse for the first and only time feels sincerely prompted to employ the language of biblical mysticism, the language of the Canticle of Canticles, of the Office of St. Agnes and the visions of Mechthild and Gertrude. In the account of her Profession she employs the traditional conventual formulas, but here they sound original and full of content: "How lovely it was, that first kiss of Jesus in my heart — it was truly a kiss of love. I knew that I was loved, and said 'I love you and I give myself to you forever.' Jesus asked for nothing, He claimed no sacrifice.... On that day it was more than a meeting; it was a complete fusion. We were no longer two for Thérèse had disappeared like a drop of water lost in the mighty ocean." The other children, seeing her face streaming with tears, assumed the thoughts of her departed mother, or of her sister who was making her profession that same day were weighing so heavily on her spirits. "It was beyond them that all the joy of Heaven had entered one small exiled heart, and that it was too frail and weak to bear it without tears."[19]

Such a fusion of hearts does not seem to come readily to many, but is there for everybody; Thérèse continually emphasizes sanctity is not for the few. If she had followed her own instincts,

---

[19] Ida Friederike Görres, *The Hidden Face: A Study of St. Thérèse of Lisieux* (San Francisco: Ignatius Press, 2003), 88-89.

the young girl would have received Holy Communion every day. The times were not right for such Eucharistic piety, however, and because of this it is all the more surprising that a priest confessor, upon Thérèse's request, gave her permission to receive four to five times per week.

> …This permission, coming straight from Our Lord, filled me with joy. In those days, I did not dare speak of my intimate feelings; but now I am quite sure one should mention to one's confessor the desire to receive Our Lord. It is not to remain alone in a golden ciborium that He comes down every day from heaven, but to find another heaven infinitely dearer to Him: the heaven of our soul, created in His image, the living temple of the adorable Trinity.[20]

On one occasion, Thérèse was ill, and the Prioress felt it beneficial for her to take medicine. It would have broken the Eucharistic fast on a day when the community was receiving. She broke into tears at the thought of being deprived of the Body of Christ — so much so that Mother Gonzague allowed her to first receive Communion, and then take the prescribed remedy. Not only did she experience sorrow over the possibility of even once being deprived of the Bread of Life, but she was of a strong mind that religious should receive the Eucharist daily. In this she was unusually ahead of her time, and her thoughts were considered a bit suspect by some in Carmel!

> "Mother, when I am dead I will make you change your mind," she said. She prayed ardently for the

---

[20] Cited in Piat, op. cit., 149.

grace that the Church might renew its former custom of permitting the faithful to receive Holy Communion at every Mass. St. Joseph, the head of the household, of whom it was said that he gave to his loved ones "food at the proper times," was her special patron in this special concern of hers. In Lisieux the great revision of ecclesiastical practice, which came about through the decrees of Pope Pius X, was ascribed in considerable part to Thérèse's intercession. A few days after her death a new priest came to the Lisieux Carmel and delivered his first sermon on the words "Come and eat my bread." Soon afterwards, with the Prioress's consent, he introduced daily Communion.[21]

The life-giving element is central in Thérèse's Eucharistic writing, but her own desire to receive Holy Communion daily was: to please Jesus Christ. The personal advantage to herself was eclipsed by her ardent desire to correspond with the plans of Merciful Love.

It was the desire to please Christ and to be nourished by Him that caused her, after receiving Our Lord, to keep repeating over and over the words of Saint Paul to the Colossians, "It is no longer I who live; Christ is living in me." She would undoubtedly encourage everyone to do the same. Making this prayer our own could be Thérèse's legacy to us! She also encourages us to…

> Remember we were not left orphans here
> When to Thy Father thou didst go, and mine;
> Thou mad'st Thyself a prisoner on earth,

---

[21] Görres, op. cit., 235-236.

Veiling the radiance of Thy light divine
And yet the veil, Dear Lord, is luminous and clear
O living Bread of faith, our food celestial here
Love's mystery! From heaven
My daily bread is given
And Jesus, it is Thou![22]

The question of an individual's worthiness enters into Thérèse's writings on the Eucharist, and clearly reflected her times. Most people felt themselves extremely unworthy, highly sinful, and properly disposed to receive Communion little more than once a year, if that. What makes her Little Way so revolutionary is the emphasis on the merciful love of God, and how this directly relates to our relationship with Him. "The guest of our soul knows our misery," she once wrote, "He comes to find an empty tent within us — that is all He asks."[23] Once, when Thérèse was Mistress of Novices, one of the young sisters under her care came to her with a serious concern she felt certain would deprive her of approaching the altar rail. "Instead of closing up the corolla of her heart," she admonished the novice, "you should open it out, that the Bread of Angels may come to nourish you, and give you all you need."[24] Her own cousin, Sister Marie of the Eucharist, was more in need of convincing. She was tortured with terrible scrupulosity which had kept her from receiving. Thérèse found she had to be kind, but also firm.

> …The Devil must indeed be clever to deceive a soul
> like that… but surely you know that this is the one goal

---

[22] Cited in Piat, op. cit., 151-152.
[23] Ibid., 152.
[24] Ibid.

of his desires. He realizes, treacherous creature that he is… that he cannot get a soul to sin if that soul belongs wholly to Jesus, so he only tries to make it think it is in sin…. Do you realize that Jesus is there expressly in the tabernacle for you? He burns with the desire to come into your heart. Don't listen to the demon — laugh at him, and go without fear to receive the Jesus of peace and love.[25]

As in so many other areas, Thérèse is not offering some overly sentimentalized view of the Eucharist. She never intended to convey the thought to anyone that, once having taken Our Lord into our souls, we would immediately experience a trans-forming union which would transport us out of the daily reality in which we are put to save our souls. In fact, she is always very careful not to confuse reality with human emotions. Too often, people who do not experience an emotional high after prayer or the reception of the sacraments, tend to blame themselves for their own lack of fervor, their lack of trying to come close to Christ. Those kinds of feelings should be set aside by anyone who reads seriously Thérèse's thoughts following her own reception of Holy Communion.

> …There is no time when I feel less consolation. Again, is that not quite natural since I do not desire the visit of the Lord for my own satisfaction, but solely for His pleasure.[26]

---

[25] Ibid., 152-153.
[26] Ibid., 152.

Much of her writing on the Eucharist was put forward by a girl of sixteen and a half years; she had been in the convent no more than one year and a half. After her death, Msgr. De Tiel, the vice postulator of her cause, brought this information to Pope Saint Pius X. The Holy Father was very impressed and said that such news was "most welcome… most opportune." He hastened to add his very personal joy and said, "We must advance her cause quickly."[27] This is the same Pope who, some years before she was actually canonized, called Thérèse "the greatest saint of modern times." He is also the Pope of the Eucharist who implemented many changes in the church's laws regarding reception of the sacrament, most notably lowering the age for First Holy Communion to the "age of reason." Given this, Father Piat's title for Thérèse, the "saint of the Eucharist," is all the more understandable. She who prayed so hard for what Pius X implemented as Pope will help us to love Our Lord truly present with us in His Body, Blood, Soul and Divinity. She who reverenced the Blessed Sacrament so much, who wrote much of her autobiography and other writings in the Eucharistic presence of Christ in the Carmel chapel will pray for us in these times of irreverence, disbelief in the real presence, and faltering faith. May Thérèse deepen in us the mystery of the Eucharistic Christ present with us, and may we, with her, never cease to thank Him for this marvelous gift!

---

[27] Ibid., 153.

CHAPTER TEN

THÉRÈSE
AND THE BLESSED VIRGIN MARY

Thérèse lost her mother when she was four and a half years of age. The impact on her would be lasting. Pauline and Marie, her two older sisters filled that role until each, in her turn, entered Carmel. Perhaps this accounts for the deep devotion the young girl cultivated at an early age to the Mother of God, and the fact that it was such an important component of the spiritual life which began with her Baptism, in the Church of Our Lady in Alençon, on January 10, 1873, one week after her birth. The uniqueness of her contribution to Marian devotion was her emphasis on Our Lady as a mother more than a queen. This does not mean she did not focus on the latter, but as her writing matured, it was the more personal, motherly aspect of Mary that preoccupied her. In this, she anticipated the Second Vatican Council by decades. The Council Fathers, in describing Mary as Mother of the Church, and by including this description within the *Dogmatic Constitution on the Church*, were teaching that Our Blessed Mother is one of us, totally sharing our humanity, though preserved from all stain of Original Sin. She is the believer par excellence, the follower of the Lord whose life we all find worthy of imitation. Thérèse knew this in the nineteenth century, and expressed it well and often in her writings.

In her autobiography, she recalled the day of her First Confession, and the role Our Lady played. She received the sacrament from Father Ducellier in the Cathedral of Saint-Pierre in Lisieux, and when Thérèse entered the box and knelt down, she was so small, it was not possible for the priest to see anyone on the other side of the screen. He asked her to stand up to receive the sacrament, and upon its reception, she experienced great delight.

> I remember the first exhortation directed to me. Father
> encouraged me to be devout to the Blessed Virgin and
> I promised myself to redouble my tenderness for her.[1]

The best remembered episode from her young life's association with Mary was her encounter with the "Virgin of the Smile." The statue which became so famous in her life, and which many still pray to, placed as it is over the saint's tomb, was one which had been in the possession of the Martin family for several years. It was a gift to Louis Martin when he was still single. Mademoiselle Felicité Baudouin had helped him set up his jewelry shop on the rue de Pont-Neuf in Alençon, and had presented him the statue when he opened his business. He placed it amidst some greenery as one entered the store, and, after his marriage to Zélie Guerin in 1858, he brought it inside their home, first on the rue de Pont-Neuf, and later on the rue de Sainte-Blaise. It became the focal point for parents and children to gather daily to pray, and on at least one occasion, after the death of her five and a half year-old daughter Hélène, Madame Martin said she

---

[1] John Clarke, OCD (trans.), *Story of a Soul: The Autobiography of Saint Thérèse of Lisieux* (Washington, DC: ICS Publications, 1996), 40-41.

received a great grace of serenity and acceptance while praying before this particular image of the Blessed Mother.

The statue's real efficacy occurred on May 13, 1883, when Thérèse claimed to be cured from the mysterious disease that had been plaguing her for some time. A novena of Masses was celebrated at the Parisian church of Our Lady of Victories, and on Pentecost Sunday…

> All of a sudden, the Blessed Virgin seemed beautiful to me, more beautiful than anything I had ever seen, her face radiated ineffable goodness and tenderness, but what penetrated to the depths of my soul was the ravishing smile of the Blessed Virgin.[2]

One of the church's preeminent theologians, Hans Urs Cardinal von Balthasar, has carefully studied this episode, in light of Thérèse's mission:

> The statue comes to life before her eyes; it becomes beautiful, more beautiful than words can express, and the Mother of God smiles, moves toward Thérèse, and cures her. It is the first 'great miracle' within Thérèse's experience. It is her first direct and inexpressibly blessed encounter with the reality of heaven, her first entry into the world of the saints; now she has seen the opening of the secret door through which one can observe the innermost secrets of God. It is her first great vision (and anyone who tries to psychologize it

---

2 Cited in Pierre Descouvemont, *Thérèse and Lisieux* (Grand Rapids, MI: Wm. B. Eerdmans Publishing Co., 1996), 52.

away has to contradict the saint's own unambiguous testimony); and so it becomes the source from which her mission springs.[3]

In later years, Thérèse would recount this event often. At first, her scrupulosity nearly got the best of her. She feared the "smile" of the Blessed Mother was only an illusion, a result of the disease from which she had suffered. It was not until a trip to the sanctuary of Our Lady of Victories in Paris at the beginning of her Roman sojourn that her fears were resolved. On May 28, 1888, she was finally relieved of all doubt when she went to confession to Father Pichon, the Jesuit to whom she had confided so much of her inner spiritual life. With such peace of mind, she could look back on the incident for what it had been, and appreciate the Blessed Mother's working in her life.

> ...How fervently I begged her to protect me always, to bring to fruition as quickly as possible my dream of hiding behind the shadow of her virginal mantle. This was one of my first desires as a child. When growing up, I understood it was at Carmel I would truly find the Blessed Virgin's mantle, and toward this fertile mount, I directed all my desires.[4]

In a school retreat prior to her First Holy Communion in 1884, she took several resolutions, one of which was to recite the *Memorare* to Our Lady every day of her life.

Hence a deep devotion was cultivated in her from early

---

[3] Hans Urs von Balthasar, *Thérèse of Lisieux: The Story of a Mission* (London: Sheed and Ward, 1953), 52.

[4] Clarke, op. cit., 123.

childhood, and would continue to grow until age fifteen when she entered Carmel, where so much of it was brought to fruition. The Order she entered in 1888 had a centuries old tradition of devotion to the Mother of God as one of its principal components.

> As a virgin, the Madonna is a model of the contemplative element in Carmelite life and also of the apostolic charism of the Order. Carmelites were found among the staunchest of defenders of the Immaculate Conception and in their spirituality they have always emphasized purity of heart as the basis of their aspiration to a life of contemplation…. In her the Carmelites saw perfectly realized the obsequium to Christ, to whom they had pledged their loyalty. The land of Carmel, for which the Carmelites have always experienced a profound nostalgia, ended up by being considered the property of Mary; its inhabitants were obliged to live in concord and to be attentive to the virtues of the Patroness…. The Carmelites believed that more than any other factor, Carmel existed to honor the Madonna. She has wanted this religious family in the Church; she has protected it and continues to protect it. The prevenient love of Mary as patroness and mother guarantees a dynamic and creative presence of Mary, but it should be completed by an increasingly ardent response…. The Marian title that is best loved and most frequently used in Carmel is that of Mother.[5]

---

[5] Redemptus Valabek, O.Carm., "Carmelite Spirituality," in Emeterio de Cea, OP (ed.), *Compendium of Spirituality*, Vol. II. (Staten Island, NY: Alba House, 1992), 166-167.

The Mother of Christ was seen as the example of the perfect disciple and servant of the Lord, worthy of emulation by every member of Carmel. This was the Order Thérèse entered on April 9, 1888, the feast of the Annunciation of the Blessed Virgin Mary, transferred that year because of the feast of Easter. The following year, she wrote to her cousin Marie Guerin, who would later enter Carmel, encouraging her to…

> Have no fear of loving the Blessed Virgin too much. You will never love her enough, and Jesus will be pleased, since the Blessed Virgin is His mother.[6]

In Carmel, Thérèse lived constantly under the watchful eye of Our Lady. There was a prominent statue in the cloister walk that bore a striking resemblance to the Virgin of the Smile of Les Buissonets. In Thérèse's works, there are two hundred thirty-nine allusions to Mary, eight of the fifty-four poems she wrote in her convent years were dedicated to the Blessed Mother, and she is mentioned in sixteen more. As a religious, one of her favorite depictions of Mary was of her holding the Divine Child, who is holding another child in His arms. This seemed to capture what Thérèse wanted to teach in her Little Way, that the more one makes oneself little, the more Mary can lead one to Jesus. She wrote about it in one of her Christmas poems.

> I will hide you under the veil
> Where the King of Heaven is sheltered
> My son will be the only star
> To shine henceforth before your eyes

---

[6] Thérèse to Marie Guerin, May 30, 1889. Cited in Eamon Carroll, "Thérèse and the Mother of God," in John Sullivan, OCD (ed.), *Carmelite Studies: Experiencing St. Thérèse Today* (Washington, DC: ICS Publications, 1990), 86.

> But that I might always shelter you
> Under my veil, close to Jesus,
> You must remain little
> Adorned with childlike virtues.[7]

Thérèse was professed on the feast of the Nativity of the Blessed Virgin Mary, September 8, 1890, and sent out an invitation to family and friends which alerted them they were being invited to her spiritual espousal to Christ by "God Almighty, creator of Heaven and Earth, Sovereign Ruler of the Universe, and the Most Glorious Virgin Mary, Queen of the Heavenly Court."[8] It indicated the formal nature of the event, and seems almost out of keeping with her continual emphasis on Mary's motherhood. One year earlier, in July, 1889, in the midst of her novitiate year, the Saint received, what was to her, a unique Marian grace.

> It was like a veil thrown over all the things of earth for me.... I was entirely hidden under the Blessed Virgin's veil. At that time, I was in charge of the refectory, and I remember that I was doing things as if I weren't doing them: it was as if I had been lent a body. I remained this way for an entire week.[9]

The theme of being covered by the Blessed Mother's veil was repeated in this verse:

> O Immaculate Virgin! You are my sweet star
> Who gives me Jesus and unites me to Him

---

[7] Cited in Descouvement, op. cit., 152.

[8] Clarke, op. cit., 168.

[9] Cited in Descouvement, op. cit., 152.

> O Mother, let me rest under your veil
> Only for today.[10]

Another telling aspect of Thérèse's Marian piety was her attraction to images of the Virgin and Child. In 1894, she requested her sister Céline to paint a portrait based on Raphael's *Granduca Madonna*. It depicts the Divine Child being nursed by His mother, and is not signed by the artist, but bears the inscription, "Carmel de Lisieux." In her cell, Thérèse kept a picture of Mary with the Christ Child on her knee. She always marveled that divinity humbled Himself to need motherly milk to be nourished; in a similar fashion, Thérèse considered the virginal milk necessary for the believer to be found in the Eucharist, the very body of Christ that Mary had nourished with her virginal milk.

When, at the suggestion of her sister Marie, and under the vow of obedience to her prioress, she began her autobiography, she was clear that...

> Before taking up my pen, I knelt before the statue of Mary (the one which has given so many proofs of maternal preferences of Heaven's Queen for our family), and I begged her to guide my hand, that it trace no line displeasing to her.[11]

The very last lines she wrote, on September 8, 1897, three weeks before her death, were on the back of a Holy Card of Our Lady of Victories:

---

[10] Ibid.
[11] Clarke, op. cit., 13.

…O Mary, if I were the Queen of Heaven and you were Thérèse, I should want to be Thérèse, that you might be the Queen of Heaven.[12]

Much of what we know of Thérèse's teaching on Our Blessed Mother comes to us from a twenty-five stanza poem she wrote in May, 1897, amid great illness and duress of soul. She confided to her sister Marie that "my little canticle expresses all I think about the Blessed Virgin and all I would preach about her if I were a priest."[13] She titled her poem, "Why I love you, Mary," and one of her foremost biographers, Bishop Guy Gaucher, has called it "her Marian Testament."[14] Thérèse had read and studied much on Our Lady, and one month before her death, she told Mother Agnes that much of what she had encountered had not moved her a great deal.

Let the priests, then, show us practicable virtues! It's good to speak of her privileges, but it's necessary above all that we can imitate her. She prefers imitation to admiration, and her life was so simple! However good a sermon is on the Blessed Virgin, if we are obliged all the time to say: Ah!… Ah!… we grow tired. How I like singing to her.[15]

---

[12] Cited in F.J. Sheed (trans.), *Collected Letters of Saint Thérèse of Lisieux* (New York: Sheed and Ward, 1949), 370.

[13] John Clarke, OCD (trans.), *St. Thérèse of Lisieux: Her Last Conversations* (Washington, DC: ICS Publications, 1977), 235.

[14] Guy Gaucher, OCD, *The Story of a Life: St. Thérèse of Lisieux* (San Francisco: HarperCollins, 1993), 184.

[15] Clarke, *Last Conversations*, op. cit., 166.

Thérèse wanted to leave a lasting legacy of "singing to her," by stressing two important themes: the sufferings Our Blessed Mother endured, and the ordinariness of her life. In doing so, she emphasizes Our Lady's solidarity with all believers, and how much she is a mother, individually, to each believer. The Church has always taught we were spiritually begotten of Mary at the foot of the Cross, the Church Fathers emphasized it in their writings, and Thérèse seems to have wanted to bring out the point for all. Her emphasis on Our Lady's sufferings, beginning with the prophecy of Simeon, and concluding on Calvary, no doubt reflects her own spiritual condition three months before her death.

> For a child to love the mother, it is necessary that they share sorrows… to believe that I am your child is not difficult, for I see you are mortal and suffering like me.[16]

Her doubts of faith are clearly evident as she writes

> …Now I understand the mystery of the Temple. Mother, your beloved Child wants you to be the example of the soul who searches for Him in the night of faith…. The King of Heaven wished that His mother be plunged into the night in anguish of heart. Mary, is it therefore a good thing to suffer on earth? Yes, to suffer and love at the same time, that is the greatest happiness.[17]

---

[16] Cited in Carroll, op. cit., 91.
[17] Ibid., 92.

One could suffer and endure a great deal in the belief that he or she was being aided by one who had endured much the same in her own earthly life. Thérèse notes that in the hidden life of Nazareth, there were no miracles, no raptures, no ecstasies; rather, it was a life much like the human lives we all lead.

> …The little ones can raise their eyes to Our Lady without fear, for it is by the ordinary way, incomparable Mother, that it pleased you to walk, in order to guide us to heaven.[18]

It is to Mary, a woman of faith, raised in the ordinary circumstances of life, that Saint Thérèse, a great soul, asks all of us little souls to turn — to a mother as real as our earthly mother — a mother who has suffered herself, and will guide us through all the sufferings we are asked to endure.

> You love us, Mary, as Jesus loves us… the Savior gave us to you as the refuge of sinners when He died on the cross, to await us in heaven.[19]

---

[18] Ibid., 93.
[19] Ibid., 94.

CHAPTER ELEVEN

THE CHURCH'S DOCTOR FOR THE THIRD MILLENNIUM

Twentieth century Popes have made some very interesting comments about Thérèse. One of the most quoted is Pius X's observation that she was the greatest saint of modern times — this some ten years before she was canonized! His successor, Benedict XV felt that she and her works should not be kept hidden from a single one of the faithful, while Pius XI, who canonized her in 1925, considered her the star of his Pontificate, and was said never to have made a significant decision without first turning to her in prayer. Her relics remained continually on his desk, and he believed that she had acquired such a knowledge of and intimacy with the supernatural, that whatever she wrote was nearly akin to the living word of God. Pope Pius XII, so close to our own times, contrasted the hidden nature of her life with the effect of her message, believing God had so intended it since, from the silence of her cloister, she was in a far more advantageous position to have a powerful effect on the entire world. Blessed John XXIII had a natural affinity to the Church's first woman Doctor, Teresa of Avila, Thérèse's patron, but if the two were held up to comparison, John felt Thérèse would bring us safely to shore, and very quickly. Such papal sentiments all had something in common; it was a deep appreciation for the doctrine Thérèse gave to the world, the way of spiritual childhood, the way of supernatural confidence. New York's Bishop Ahern put it succinctly:

> The point is that as time has passed Thérèse has come to be seen not so much as someone who answers prayers, though she still does so quite dramatically, but rather as one of the most outstanding mystics in the history of the church. Far more than for the power of her intercession, she is known for the depth of her insight into the mystery of who God is. She knew God deeply because she loved Him deeply. 'How can I FEAR A God,' she asked, "who is nothing but mercy and love?" That was her definition of God: 'nothing but mercy and love.' Everything else in the Little Way and in her spiritual doctrine follows from that profound intuition.[1]

Abbé André Combes, one of the great Thérèsian scholars of his era, tried to capture what he called her spirit and message for the world. Combes was fully aware of the growing sentiment to have her proclaimed a Doctor of the Church. He looked closely at her life, and saw its particulars as a series of abrupt, unpredictable changes, rather than a logical, orderly unfolding. Its most important facets are covered by each of her major biographers: the "Virgin of the Smile," who, she claimed, cured her at the age of ten; her First Communion, and the beginning of a deep Eucharistic life; her Christmas "conversion" of 1886; her devotion to

---

[1] Patrick V. Ahern, "Thérèse, Doctor of the Church," *Origins*, Vol. 27, No. 12, September 4, 1997, 194.

the Precious Blood of Christ, brought on by her gazing at a picture of the Crucifixion; from April of 1888, her long "martyrdom of Divine love," her conception of a new spiritual teaching — a "lift" to heaven; her 1893 instructions to her novices, demanding of them their fixed attention on the supernatural; her poems on the interior life; her 1895 Act of Oblation to the merciful love of God; her autobiography, *The Story of a Soul*; her terrible trial of faith; her excruciating illness, and her death. Putting these together, culling from them, and trying to discern her spirit and message, Combes focused on three areas, or themes, with which most Thérèsian scholars would agree.

Thérèse's first spiritual legacy, said Combes, was her belief that everything is a grace. As she looked back on the many physical, emotional and spiritual struggles she was asked to endure, she accepted them all as God's gifts to her. In a real sense, it was like saying "yes" to a life of ongoing martyrdom — not unlike Our Lady's "yes" to the will of God expressed in the Annunciation. She had been tested long and hard, and she realized she was not alone; everyone is called on to endure suffering in some way, everyone is being purified through some process or other. Much as Juliana of Norwich, the mediaeval mystic said that for the just man all would be well, so Thérèse saw this same result for all those, no matter what the character of their lives had been, who accept all happenings as part of God's providential plan.

Secondly, the saint teaches that holiness is a disposition of the heart. One month before her death, Thérèse's sister, Mother Agnes, spoke very sincerely from her own heart, expressing her admiration for her, and her belief that her younger sister had already reached a very high degree of sanctity, given all she had been asked to endure. Thérèse made her famous reply:

Oh! — it's not that!… Holiness does not consist in this
or that practice, but in a disposition of heart, by which
we rest humbly in the arms of God as His little children, conscious of our weakness, yet boldly confident
in the goodness of our Father.[2]

Thérèse was never conspicuous for fasting, mortification,
penances, etc., beyond what the rule of Carmel called for (that
was severe enough by any human reckoning, and Thérèse kept it
with particular diligence). She knew that going off on one's own
with such practices was not the way to become a saint. This is
not to suggest that holiness is a work of God alone, that we have
nothing to do with it. Holiness is a very human thing, according
to Thérèse, though no human effort of ours can bring it about;
rather, it follows from her first step. If everything is a grace, the
action of God's love comes first. Our response to that divine
initiative is to abandon ourselves totally to it. We must place
ourselves completely in the hands of the God who loves us, fully
cognizant of our weakness, our failings, and our sins. Only with
this disposition do our actions have any real power to sanctify us.
Holiness, then, is a disposition of the will which, realizing its own
powerlessness, accepts the workings of God. From the moment a
person realizes that everything is a grace, and yields the entirety
of his or her life to God, that person has entered into the mystical
order. Once there, the person is totally receptive to the plan God
has for him or her, and God, in turn, will expect acts of virtue to
flow from each life. Abbé Combes, who has analyzed the thought
of Thérèse so well, explains what these acts of virtue might be:

---

[2] Cited in Abbé André Combes, *The Spirituality of Saint Thérèse: An Introduction* (New
York: P.J. Kenedy and Sons, 1950), 150.

Perhaps it is a rich outburst of works of sanctity; perhaps it is a long monotonous journey which never seems to rise above mediocrity; perhaps it is the inner martyrdom of the soul.[3]

In any event, it is in lives and situations known to all of us that holiness is achieved, and this is the true road to spiritual childhood that no one teaches us better than Thérèse.

This leads to the final point of her doctrine; to love, to be loved, and to make love loved. She made this point one day to her sister Céline. The latter was reading to her during her final illness, and she had chosen a passage from a spiritual work which described the beauty of the beatific vision in heaven. Thérèse said that was not what most preoccupied her; rather, it was loving God, being loved by Him. And doing this in the course of the particular vocation He had chosen for her in this world. God had meant everything to her in this life, and she wanted to overcome the tremendous ingratitude she found all about her; she wanted to win all hearts to the merciful love of God, and she set herself to that task, not only for the years God permitted her to remain in this world, but until time is no more. This, in essence, is the spiritual doctrine that would be studied in detail during the century which elapsed from her death until Pope John Paul II officially proclaimed her the thirty-third Doctor of the Church.

One becomes a Doctor of the Church by fulfilling three requirements: having a holiness of life which was truly outstanding, even among saints; possessing a depth of doctrinal content, and leaving an extensive body of writings which the Church can recommend to its members as free from error and true to authentic

---
[3] Ibid., 153.

THE SAINT FOR THE THIRD MILLENNIUM: THÉRÈSE OF LISIEUX

tradition. No one would ever question Thérèse's holiness; and, to fulfill the second requirement, one scholar has noted that "she has sounded the depth of God's merciful love as perhaps no saint has done before."[4] Thirdly, in her writings, she produced extensive prose, poetry, voluminous correspondence, and her classic autobiography.

Organized, vocal appeals for Thérèse to be declared a Doctor of the Church began in earnest following her canonization in 1925. Seven years later, at the inauguration of the crypt church of the basilica in Lisieux, there was held the "Great Congress," at which a French Jesuit, Father Desbuquois, a leading member of the Catholic Action Populaire, delivered a long-remembered lecture, looking to the future, and the possibility of such a declaration. He, with the help of others, put together a theological dossier, to which contributions from around the world advanced arguments for her case. This file finally arrived at the desk of Pope Pius XI. The feeling was one of great optimism, since this Pope had both beatified and canonized Thérèse, and declared her Co-Patroness of the Missions along with Saint Francis Xavier. But apparently he felt the time was not opportune for a woman to be declared one of the Church's Doctors. He had previously turned down a similar appeal on behalf of Saint Teresa of Avila, further underscoring the inappropriateness of such a declaration in the early decades of the twentieth century. For his part, Father Desbuquois confided to the saint's sister, Mother Agnes of Jesus, his strong belief that her sister would one day be accorded such an honor. The Jesuit died in 1959, far in advance of the papacy of John Paul II, but one must believe that in the Communion of Saints, he continued to do his part.

---

[4]   Ahern, op. cit., 193.

The "storm of glory" that Lisieux witnessed, as well as the personal devotion not only of the French people, but also of so many others around the world, gives additional testimony that calls for her advancement would continue. It is said that the majority of French soldiers during the First World War carried her picture, and of these, no one was more conspicuous than Henri Giralou.

Giralou saw heavy action in the war and, until the end of his life, believed he had come through the fighting unharmed because of Thérèse's intercession. Soon after, he became a Carmelite and rose to high positions in the Order. He was an especially well known preacher, an expert on Carmelite spirituality, and a founder of the Secular Institute of Notre Dame de Vie. In religion, he was known as Father Marie-Eugene of the Child Jesus, and he devoted his entire priestly life to making Thérèse and her Little Way better known. In 1947, he delivered a lecture in which he described Thérèse as a "Doctor of the Mystical Life." While this was the first time such a title had been so conspicuously applied to her, Father Marie-Eugene contended that it "in no sense anticipates any possible move on the part of the Church to rank Saint Thérèse among her Doctors."[5] Nonetheless, he contended that both historians and theologians would do well to study her life, to discover that, in becoming a Carmelite through and through, she became a saint, not to mention a master of the spiritual life. "It was in climbing Mount Carmel with love," he noted, "that she discovered the way of spiritual childhood and traced out its paths so luminously."[6] She did so by what he described as the spirit of Elijah, the discipline of Teresa of Avila and the doctrine of John of the Cross.

---

[5] Father Marie-Eugene of the Child Jesus, *Under the Torrent of His Love* (New York: Alba House, 1995), 63.

[6] Ibid., 69.

Elijah, the Old Testament prophet, is considered the father of Carmel. He was snatched away from his family to do the works of God, and a tremendous love of God was put into his soul. He followed God's command to go to the desert, and was ultimately called to fulfill the mission of caring for God's people Israel. Elijah's task was not an easy one; and he carried it out amidst great pain. In like manner, Thérèse was caught up in the love of God, the same sort of zeal ignited her soul, and she had a specific mission — internally to save souls and especially the souls of priests through her prayers, and externally to spend her heaven doing good on earth. She did this with the same discipline Saint Teresa of Avila knew well. By her meticulous observance of the Carmelite rule, she lived out, day after day, the teaching of the saint she saw as her spiritual mother. But, said Father Marie-Eugene, it was the doctrine of John of the Cross which impacted on her most forcefully.[7] She found in his writings a climate not unlike her own, and a teaching that made her own dark night of the soul seem quite bearable. After climbing the mount of Carmel with the help of these three:

> Saint Thérèse of the Child Jesus does not bring us any new revelations or new theological conclusions. Everyone will agree with this, I hope, and rejoice in it.... It seems to me that the newness consists in this: Thérèse... saw God and Christianity with the pure, fresh eyes of a child. She realized... with rigorous and absolute logic what her child's eye had discovered, and then expressed it with a simplicity and candid sincerity which, again, belong to a child.

---

[7] For the most thorough treatment of John of the Cross' influence on Thérèse, see Guy Gaucher, *John and Thérèse: Flames of Love* (New York: Alba House, 1999).

She was not a great theologian in the strict sense…

> But if we can define spiritual theology as that science which orders all things in the light of God and His Christ, and directs man's steps wisely to his last end, then there is no doubt, that Thérèse is a great spiritual theologian.

Father Marie-Eugene concludes:

> Her gaze penetrated God to such depths, and she saw with such pure clarity the path leading to Him, that she was able to express her discoveries in the simple language of a child. She possessed the science of salvation to a high degree and was able to impart it with rare perfection.[8]

That was in 1947. Twenty-three years would pass before Pope Paul VI declared the first two women Doctors of the Church: Teresa of Avila and Catherine of Siena. His initiative was prophetic, and three years later, the theologian and future Cardinal Hans Urs von Balthasar, speaking at the centenary celebrations of Thérèse's birth, asked rhetorically if she could one day be declared a Doctor. "My reply is yes," he said, "and without hesitation."[9]

A few years before Thérèse was named a Doctor, Bishop Patrick V. Ahern offered a number of compelling reasons for such a course. Thérèse knew the same world we know, one of science and technology, in which many do not believe in God because

---

[8] Father Marie-Eugene, op. cit., 98-99.

[9] Cited in Interview of Msgr. Guy Gaucher, Auxiliary Bishop of Bayeux and Lisieux, *Union Sacerdotale de Sainte Thérèse de Lisieux* (Lisieux: Direction du Pelerinage de Lisieux, n. 10, October, 1997), 55.

they intellectually attempt to explain Him away. In fact, she often prayed for atheists, and for all those who in any way despaired or were seriously tormented; she knew the feeling well, was tempted to suicide during her final illness, and often expressed wonderment that more people did not commit suicide when they were in the throes of such agony. Thérèse was one of us in her serious doubts of faith — though she clung to that faith "with the courage of a thousand martyrs and against all kinds of odds."[10] She is one of us moderns in her battle with neurosis, and in the way in which she watched her father, "whom she all but adored," spend nearly four years of his life in a mental institution. In Thérèse, we can see ourselves with "our poor human weakness and all the onslaughts of anxiety which many of us endure."[11] Finally, we need another woman Doctor of the Church, one who "in the best of times and the worst of times" said she sought nothing but the truth, and never ceased to proclaim it.

> It is not for the honor of Thérèse that we seek her doctorate, for she needs no honors. We seek it for our own need. By placing her in the doctor's chair and putting on her shoulders the doctor's gown, the church will call us all to sit at the feet of this astonishing young woman, to restudy the Gospel and be filled anew with its light.[12]

The Vatican has always held the process of declaring a Doctor of the Church in strict confidence; still, the Catholic press in the United States was able to gather some important information

---

[10] Ahern, op. cit., 195.
[11] Ibid.
[12] Ibid.

and report on it. Some years after the conferral of her doctorate, at least one serious, in-depth work appeared detailing the process.[13] Initially, the Congregation for Saints accepted a positio, a large file of nearly one thousand pages with arguments and facts on the "eminent doctrine" of Saint Thérèse, and her influence on the universal Church. Pope John Paul II received hundreds of letters from Catholics around the world asking that he declare her a Doctor. On May 5, 1997, the Congregation for the Doctrine of the Faith held a final session to consider whether Saint Thérèse's writings could be considered truly eminent. Three weeks later, the Congregation for the Causes of Saints carried out a similar scrutiny, and in both cases, majorities gave full consent, with few dissenting votes. Thirty-five priests, bishops and cardinals were brought together, a vote was taken, and the outcome was unanimous. Saint Thérèse could be considered a great teacher of the faith, and fully met the first two requirements to be named a Doctor: holiness and writing. The judgment went to Pope John Paul II, and in August, 1997, he announced his decision at World Youth Day in Paris, that on Mission Sunday, October 19, 1997, he would declare Thérèse a Doctor of the Church.

In the course of his Apostolic Letter, John Paul explained that even though Thérèse does not have a well-structured doctrinal corpus, nonetheless, a "particular radiance of doctrine" is to be found in her work, a clear manifestation of the working of the Holy Spirit in and through her.

The core of her message is actually the mystery of God — Love itself, of the Triune God, infinitely perfect

---

[13] The most thoroughly researched work on the Doctorate of Thérèse is Steven Payne, OCD, *Saint Thérèse of Lisieux: Doctor of the Universal Church* (New York: Alba House, 2002).

in Himself. If genuine Christian spiritual experience should conform to the revealed truths in which God communicates Himself and the mystery of His will (cf. *Dei Verbum*, n. 2), it must be said that Thérèse experienced divine revelation, going so far as to contemplate the fundamental truths of our faith united in the mystery of Trinitarian life. At the summit, as the source and goal, is the merciful love of the three Divine Persons, as she expresses it, especially in her Act of Oblation to Merciful Love. At the basis, on the subject's part, is the experience of being the Father's adoptive children in Jesus; this is the most authentic meaning of spiritual childhood: that is, the experience of divine filiation, under the motion of the Holy Spirit. At the basis again, and standing before us, is our neighbor, are others, for whose salvation we must collaborate with and in Jesus, with the same merciful love as His.

Through spiritual childhood one experiences that everything comes from God, returns to Him and abides in Him, for the salvation of all, in a mystery of merciful love. Such is the doctrinal message taught and lived by this Saint.[14]

Hence, the spotlight has been turned on Thérèsian spirituality, a sharp focus is given to what Thérèse intended to teach the world. She is on an equal plane with thirty-two other Doctors of the Church, each of whom has a unique teaching and defense of the faith to offer the entire Mystical Body of Christ as we sojourn

---

[14] Pope John Paul II, *Apostolic Letter: Saint Thérèse of the Child Jesus and the Holy Face Is Proclaimed Doctor of the Universal Church* (Strasbourg: Editions du Signe, 1997), 27.

through this world. In the case of the Church's newest Doctor, the more one studies her, the more one is called…

> To rediscover a theology made on the knees, which not only nourishes the mind, but satisfies the whole being, helps it to find its inner unity.… [Hers is] the reality of an intense mystical life in daily life, in the present moment, always in contact with what is basic to daily human existence.[15]

Millions of people have discovered that spirituality in the one hundred ten years since Thérèse's death. It is a way of life that seems to be coming more and more into its own. When Thérèse predicted that the whole world would love her, she was not making some sort of egotistical statement. It was not directed at her at all. She meant that the merciful love of God, which she did so much to emphasize, would be appreciated and loved by generation after generation. Her popularity grows with each passing year because her message reaches countless numbers. Her autobiography has been translated into all the major languages of the world, and ranks among the best known pieces of spiritual literature. Tangible proof of this will be found no more convincingly than in a pilgrimage to that famous town in Normandy so closely associated with her life.

> More than a million people pass through Lisieux each year. Pilgrims and tourists of all ages, from all classes of society, from all countries. In the chapel of the Carmel, and at Les Buissonets, metal workers rub shoulders with

---

[15] Gaucher Interview, op. cit., 59-61.

lawyers, Japanese intellectuals with sinners from Pigalle, a North African Muslim with a Belgian missionary, the French country family with a South American theologian, a group of German pilgrims with Canadian religious, the Orthodox Christian who informs you that the only Western saints the Russians venerate are Francis of Assisi and Thérèse of Lisieux.[16]

Saint Thérèse, then, is one we can all put to work for us. She once said she could never rest while there were souls to save, and only when the Angel said time was no more would she take her rest. What so many souls, prominent and unknown, have discovered about Thérèse in the past one hundred ten years, you and I can just as easily discover, and appreciate, in our own time. "In the end her mystery eludes us," wrote Bishop Guy Gaucher, "but isn't it better that way?"[17]

---

[16] Guy Gaucher, *The Story of a Life: St. Thérèse of Lisieux* (San Francisco: HarperCollins, 1993), 216.

[17] Ibid.

BIBLIOGRAPHY

Books

Ahern, Patrick V. *Maurice and Thérèse: The Story of a Love*. New York: Doubleday, 1998.

_____. *St. Thérèse: Patroness of the Missions*. New York: The Society for the Propagation of the Faith, undated.

Baaudoin-Croix, Marie. *Leonie Martin: A Difficult Life*. Dublin: Veritas, 1993.

Beevers, John. *Storm of Glory: St. Thérèse of Lisieux*. London: Sheed and Ward, 1950.

Bro, Bernard, O.P. *The Little Way: The Spirituality of Thérèse of Lisieux*. London: Darton, Longman and Todd, 1979.

Catechism of the Catholic Church. Liguori, MO: Liguori Publications, 1994.

Cavanaugh, Arthur. *Thérèse: The Saint Who Loved Us*. Mahwah, NJ: Paulist Press, 2003.

Cavnar, Cindy (ed.) *Prayers and Meditations of Thérèse of Lisieux*. Ann Arbor, MI: Servant Publications, 1992.

Clarke, John, O.C.D. (trans.). *St. Thérèse of Lisieux: Her Last Conversations*. Washington, DC: ICS Publications, 1977.

_____. *Story of a Soul: The Autobiography of St. Thérèse of Lisieux*. Washington, DC: ICS Publications, 1996.

Coady, Mary Frances. *The Hidden Way: The Life and Influence of Almire Pichon*. Toronto: Novalis, 1998.

Combes, André. *The Heart of St. Thérèse*. Dublin: M.H. Gill and Son, Ltd., 1952.

_____. *The Spirituality of St. Thérèse: An Introduction*. New York: P.J. Kenedy and Sons, 1950.

_____. *St. Thérèse and Suffering: The Spirituality of St. Thérèse in its Essence*. Dublin: M.H. Gill and Son, Ltd., 1951.

_____. *Saint Thérèse and Her Mission: The Basic Principles of Thérèsian Spirituality*. Dublin: M.H. Gill and Son, Ltd., 1956.

Day, Dorothy. *Thérèse*. Springfield, IL: Templegate Publishers, 1991.

Day, Michael (ed.). *Christian Simplicity in St. Thérèse: The Place of St. Thérèse of Lisieux in Christian Spirituality*. London: Burns Oates, 1953.

D'Elbée, Jean C.J. *I Believe in Love: A Personal Retreat Based on the Teachings of St. Thérèse of Lisieux*. Manchester, NH: Sophia Institute Press, 2001.

De La Vierge, Victor, O.C.D. *Spiritual Realism of Saint Thérèse of Lisieux*. St. Helens, Lancashire: Wood, Westworth & Co., Ltd., 1960.

De Meester, Conrad, O.C.D. *The Power of Confidence: Genius and Structure of the "Way of Spiritual Childhood" of St. Thérèse of Lisieux*. New York: Alba House, 1998.

_____. *With Empty Hands: The Message of St. Thérèse of Lisieux*. Washington, DC: ICS Publications, 2002.

De Cea, Emeterio, O.P. (ed.). *Compendium of Spirituality*. New York: Alba House, 1996, 2 Volumes.

Descouvemont, Pierre. *Thérèse and Lisieux*. Grand Rapids, MI: Wm. B. Eerdmans Publishing Co., 1991.

_____. *Thérèse of Lisieux and Marie of the Trinity: The transformative relationship of St. Thérèse of Lisieux and her novice Sister Marie of the Trinity*. New York: Alba House, 1997.

Ducrocq, Marie-Pascale. *Thérèse of Lisieux: A Vocation of Love*. New York: Alba House, 2000.

Durand, Msgr. G. *Histoire de la Basilique*. Lisieux: Les Annales de Sainte Thérèse de Lisieux, 1970.

Ficocelli, Elizabeth. *Shower of Heavenly Roses: Stories of Intercession of St. Thérèse of Lisieux*. New York: The Crossroad Publishing Company, 2004.

Frost, Christine. *A Guide to the Normandy of Saint Thérèse*. Birmingham, England: The Thérèsian Trust, 1994.

Gaucher, Guy, O.C.D. *John and Thérèse: Flames of Love*. New York: Alba House, 1999.

_____. *The Passion of Thérèse of Lisieux*. New York: The Crossroad Publishing Company, 1998.

_____. *The Story of a Life: St. Thérèse of Lisieux*. San Francisco: HarperCollins, 1987.

Gehon, Henri. *The Secret of the Little Flower*. London: Sheed and Ward, 1934.

Guitton, Jean. *The Spiritual Genius of Saint Thérèse of Lisieux*. Liguori, MO: Triumph Books, 1997.

Görres, Ida Friederike. *The Hidden Face: A Study of St. Thérèse of Lisieux*. San Francisco: Ignatius Press, 2003.

Herbstrith, Waltraud, O.C.D. *Edith Stein: A Biography*. San Francisco: Ignatius Press, 1992.

Horsfield, Msgr. Francis. *A Lisieux Retreat*. Addlestone, Surrey, England: Kazaphani Press, 1996.

Jamart, François, O.C.D. *Complete Spiritual Doctrine of St. Thérèse of Lisieux*. New York: Alba House, 1961; 14th printing 2001.

Johnson, Vernon. *Spiritual Childhood: The Spirituality of St. Thérèse of Lisieux*. San Francisco: Ignatius Press, 2001.

Keyes, Frances Parkinson. *St. Thérèse of Lisieux*. London: Eyre and Spottiswoode, 1950.

_____. *Written in Heaven: The Making of a Saint*. London: Eyre and Spottiswoode, Ltd., 1945.

Knox, Ronald (trans.). *Autobiography of a Saint: Thérèse of Lisieux*. Glasgow: William Collins Sons & Co., Ltd., 1958.

Lavielle, Msgr. August Pierre. *Life of the Little Flower: St. Thérèse of Lisieux*. New York: McMullen Books, Inc., 1953.

Marie-Eugene of the Child Jesus. *Under the Torrent of His Love: Thérèse of Lisieux, A Spiritual Genius*. New York: Alba House, 1995.

McCaffrey, Eugene, O.C.D. *Heart of Love: Saint Thérèse of Lisieux*. Dublin: Veritas, 1998.

_____. *The Fire of Love: Praying with Thérèse of Lisieux*. Norwich, Norfolk, England: Canterbury Press, 1998.

Morton, J.B. *St. Thérèse of Lisieux: The Making of a Saint*. London: The Catholic Book Club, 1956.

Nevins, Albert J., M.M. (ed.). *The Maryknoll Catholic Dictionary*. New York: Grosset & Dunlap, 1965.

Novissima Verba: The Last Conversations and Confidences of Saint Thérèse of the Child Jesus: May-September, 1897. Dublin: M.H. Gill and Son Ltd., 1953.

O'Connor, Patricia. *The Inner Life of Thérèse of Lisieux*. Huntington, IN: Our Sunday Visitor Publishing Division, 1997.

O'Donnell, Christopher, O.Carm. *Love in the Heart of the Church: The Mission of Thérèse of Lisieux*. Dublin: Veritas, 1997.

_____. *Prayer: Insights from St. Thérèse of Lisieux*. Dublin: Veritas, 2001.

O'Mahoney, Christopher (ed.). *St. Thérèse of Lisieux by Those who Knew Her*. Dublin: Veritas, 1975.

Payne, Steven, O.C.D. *Saint Thérèse of Lisieux: Doctor of the Universal Church*. New York: Alba House, 2002.

Petitot, Henry, O.P. *Saint Teresa of Lisieux: A Spiritual Renasence*. London: Burns, Oates & Washburne Ltd., 1927.

Piat, Stéphane-Joseph, O.F.M. *Celine: Sister Genevieve of the Holy Face*. San Francisco: Ignatius Press, 1997.

_____. *The Story of a Family: The Home of St. Thérèse of Lisieux*. Rockford, IL: TAN Books and Publishers, Inc., 1994.

Pope John Paul II. *Apostolic Letter: Saint Thérèse of the Child Jesus and the Holy Face Is proclaimed Doctor of the Universal Church*. Strasbourg: Editions Du Signe, 1997.

Redmond, Paulinus. *Louis and Zelie Martin: The Seed and the Root of the Little Flower*. London: Quiller Press Limited, 1995.

Sackville-West, V. *The Eagle and the Dove: A Study in Contrasts*. London: Michael Joseph Ltd., 1943.

Schreck, Alan. *The Compact History of the Catholic Church*. Ann Arbor, MI: Servant Books, 1987.

Sheed, F.J. (trans.). *Collected Letters of St. Thérèse of Lisieux*. New York: Sheed & Ward, 1949.

Sheen, Fulton J. *Seven Words of Jesus and Mary*. Liguori, MO: Liguori Publications, 2001.

The Spirit of Sainte Thérèse de l'Enfant Jesus. London: Burns Oates & Washburne, Ltd., 1948.

St. Thérèse: Doctor of the Little Way. New Bedford, MA: Franciscan Friars of the Immaculate, 1997.

The Story of the Canonization of St. Thérèse of Lisieux. London: Burns Oates & Washburne, Ltd., 1933.

Sullivan, John, O.C.D. *Carmelite Studies: Experiencing St. Thérèse Today*. Washington, DC: ICS Publications, 1990.

Taylor, Thomas N. *Saint Thérèse of Lisieux, the Little Flower of Jesus*. New York: P.J. Kenedy & Sons, 1927.

Tonnelier, Constant. *Fifteen Days of Prayer with Saint Thérèse of Lisieux*. Liguori, MO: Liguori Publications, 1999.

_____. *Through the Year with Saint Thérèse of Lisieux: Living the Little Way*. Liguori, MO: Liguori Publications, 1998.

Union of Priests of St. Thérèse of Lisieux: Orientations and Statutes. Lisieux, 1992.

Von Balthasar, Hans Urs. *Thérèse of Lisieux: The Story of a Mission*. London: Sheed and Ward, 1953.

_____. *Two Sisters in the Spirit: Thérèse of Lisieux and Elizabeth of the Trinity*. San Francisco: Ignatius Press, 1992.

Williamson, Benedict. *The Doctrinal Mission and Apostolate of S. Thérèse of Lisieux*. London: Alexander Ouseley Limited, 1932, 3 Volumes.

Articles

Patrick V. Ahern. "A Teacher for Today: Why Saint Thérèse should be named a Doctor of the Church." *Spiritual Life* (40) 1994, 118-120.

_____. "The Case for St. Thérèse as a Doctor of the Church." *America* (12) August 28, 1993, 12-14.

_____. "Thérèse: An Intimate Companion." Alba House Cassettes, 1989.

_____. "Thérèse, Doctor of the Church." *Origins* (27) September 4, 1997, 193-195.

Cathal B. Daly. "Thérèse: A Saint for all Seasons." Unpublished Article, Thérèsian International Congress, 1997.

Guy Gaucher. "Saint Thérèse of Lisieux: Doctor of the Church." *Union Sacerdotale de Sainte Thérèse de Lisieux* (10) October, 1997, 52-62.

_____. "The Doctorate of Thérèse in the Perspective of the Jubilee of the Year 2000." *Union Sacerdotale de Sainte Thérèse de Lisieux* (11) June, 1998, 76-113.

"Introduction to the Correspondence of Sister Thérèse of the Child Jesus and the Holy Face and Father Adolphe Roulland (1870-1934)." *Union Sacerdotale de Sainte Thérèse de Lisieux* (11) June, 1998, 66-75.

J. Linus Ryan, O. Carm. "Saint Thérèse 'Sister and Friend' of Priests." *Celebrating the First Anniversary of Saint Thérèse Relics Visit 2001.* (Spring, 2002), 15-17.